Laws of Order

LAWS OF ORDER

A BOOK OF

HIERARCHIES,

RANKINGS,

INFRASTRUCTURES,

MEASUREMENTS,

AND SIZES

JEFF ROVIN

BALLANTINE BOOKS ■ NEW YORK

Copyright © 1992 by Jeff Rovin

All rights reserved under International and Pan-American Copyright Conventions. Published in the United States by Ballantine Books, a division of Random House, Inc., New York, and simultaneously in Canada by Random House of Canada Limited, Toronto.

Library of Congress Catalog Card Number: 91-92139

ISBN: 0-345-36585-2

Cover design by Dale Fiorillo
Text design by Beth Tondreau Design

Manufactured in the United States of America

First Edition: February 1992

10 9 8 7 6 5 4 3 2 1

Contents

"All things began in order,
so shall they end, and so
shall they begin again."
    —SIR THOMAS BROWNE,
    On Dreams

Introduction

In 1791, British statesman Edmund Burke wrote, "Good order is the foundation of all good things." Never mind that Burke's incendiary, pro-America speeches often threw the House of Commons into chaos; partisan politics will do that.

But Burke's reasoning was sound, for whether the field of endeavor is language, science, politics, the arts, or connect-the-dots, order is a prerequisite for success.

This is a book about the way that nature and civilization are organized. You won't find the longest rivers and tallest buildings here; there are almanacs and atlases aplenty for that. This book concentrates on rankings, infrastructures, and sequences, from the hierarchies in heaven to the levels of hell, from the inside of an atom to the farthest reaches of the cosmos, from the meaning of the numbers on your checks to the pecking order in Thomas More's Utopia. The one hundred and ninety-one laws are arranged in twenty-seven broad topic headings for easy reference.

We hope you find these laws of order useful as well as entertaining, and welcome suggestions for laws you might like to see in future volumes.

Laws of Order

ANIMALS

Biology Classes

The job of a scientist is to understand the physical world. Unfortunately, the more scientists understand, the more they're forced to categorize, and the more complicated the world becomes to the rest of us. For example, to the ancient Egyptians, a cat was either a pet or a goddess. Today, a cat is a member of the order *Carnivora*, of the family *Felidae*. However, this description can also be applied to tigers and lions, so you must go further down the chain, to the genus *Felis*, to place your cat. And so it goes with all living things.

In order to do a complete breakdown of any life form, here are the subdivisions you'll need:

1.	Kingdom	**11.**	Order
2.	Subkingdom	**12.**	Suborder
3.	Phylum	**13.**	Superfamily
4.	Subphylum	**14.**	Family
5.	Superclass	**15.**	Subfamily
6.	Class	**16.**	Tribe
7.	Subclass	**17.**	Genus
8.	Infraclass	**18.**	Subgenus
9.	Cohort	**19.**	Species
10.	Superorder	**20.**	Subspecies

The Food Chain

Whoever said, "It's a dog-eat-dog world" didn't know much about the food chain—that is, the pyramid of food producers and consumers.

The animals in each successive level feed on those from the level before it. And while the specifics vary from region to region—in the sea, for example, the food chains are extremely variegated (see below)—the pyramids in the forest are relatively the same worldwide.

LEVEL	CONSUMERS
First	Aphids and other plant-eating insects that feed on grasses and plants.
Second	Beetles, spiders, and other insects and arachnids.
Third	Insect-eating birds.
Fourth	Hawks, weasels, and other bird-eating carnivores.
Fifth	Lice, ticks, and other parasites.

In the sea, the pyramid can be simple, as in the icy Antarctic waters:

First	Krill that feed on diatoms, a type of algae.
Second	Blue whales that eat the krill.

Or the pyramid can be more complex, as in non-polar waters where the list of carnivorous fish grows:

First	Copepods that feed on diatoms.
Second	Anchovies.
Third	Mackerel.
Fourth	Tuna.
Fifth	Humans or sharks.

Insect Metamorphosis

As detailed as all this scientific pigeonholing can be, it's the only way we'll ever get a real understanding of the world. For instance, in *Die Verwandlung* (1915; better known as *The Metamorphosis*) by Franz Kafka (1883–1924), Gregor Samsa wakes up one morning and finds himself transformed into a giant insect. There was no egg stage, no larva stage for him—just *voila!* Big bug time.

Unlike Mr. Samsa, insects in the real world go through distinct stages to reach adulthood. There are two kinds of metamorphoses: complete and incomplete. Incomplete doesn't mean unfinished; rather, it signifies the bugs avoid some of the stages in complete metamorphoses.

COMPLETE METAMORPHOSIS: *Insects such as ants, moths, butterflies, wasps, and beetles go through this process.*

1. **EGG:** A parent can lay one egg at a time or, as in the case of the termite, ten thousand in a row.
2. **LARVA:** This refers to the young insect that hatches from the egg. A larva initially looks remarkably similar to a worm; indeed, the "worm" we are unlucky enough to find on occasion in a fruit or vegetable is actually a larva (or larvae, if we're really unlucky!).
3. **PUPA:** Upon reaching its full growth, the larva hibernates, developing a shell or "pupal case" for protection. A handful of insects, like the moth, spin a hard covering called a cocoon. The resting insect is called a pupa (except in the case of the butterfly, which is known as a chrysalis), and remains in the hibernation state for several weeks or months.
4. **ADULT:** While it was hibernating, the insect was developing its adult body parts. When the insect has matured physically, the case or cocoon cracks and the full-grown insect emerges.

INCOMPLETE METAMORPHOSIS: *This process is undergone by grasshoppers, crickets, lice, and others.*

1. **EGG:** This is the same as above.

2. **EARLY-STAGE NYMPH:** This hatched insect resembles an adult—only it's *smaller* in size. However, those insects that would normally have wings have not yet developed them.

3. **LATE-STAGE NYMPH:** At this time, the skin begins to molt, and the wings begin to bud.

4. **ADULT:** The insect is now fully grown.

This process is what gives the Mexican jumping bean its bounce. Moths lay eggs inside the seed pods of the *yerba de flecha,* or the "arrow plant." When these pods heat up, the caterpillar that has developed inside—which is currently feeding on the seed—begins to wriggle. So . . . if you buy Mexican beans for your kids, and they stop moving after a few months, don't worry. The caterpillar has eaten through and moved on . . . probably into some room of your house.

The Pecking Order of Bees

Ninety-five percent of all bees live alone. They are known, logically enough, as solitary bees—or S.O. Bees, as a local beekeeper has been known to describe them. The remaining 5 percent are social bees; they live in colonies comprised of hundreds to thousands of bees.

The pecking order in such hives is very strict, and is broken down as follows:

QUEEN BEE: The unquestioned leader, who lays eggs—often as many as two thousand a day—from early spring to late summer.

DRONES: The males, whose only function in life is, literally, to fertilize the queen. (It's a tough life.)

WORKERS: Always female, though unable to lay eggs, they fall into one of two categories:

Hive Workers: These stay at home and, depending upon their age, perform various hive-keeping functions. The older they get, the more serious their duties, which rank as follows from least to most important:

1. Cleaning out the brood cells for new eggs.
2. Feeding pollen to the larvae.
3. Feeding the queen.
4. Building new cells.
5. Receiving pollen as it reaches the hive.
6. Standing guard at the hive.
7. Leaving the nest to become a forager.

Foragers: These head into the field, taking from flowers the food necessary to feed the colony.

BOOKS AND LITERATURE

The International Standard Book Number

Those bars and numbers printed on books and other products may seem, on the surface, to be garble. Yet, the numbers—the International Standard Book Numbers—found on the inside flap or back cover tell salespeople everything they could possible wish to know about a book . . . except whether or not it's as good as the cover copy says it is!

After the letters ISBN:

1. The first number reveals the language in which the book was published. English is designated by "O."
2. The second set of numbers identifies the publisher.
3. The third group identifies that book in particular. Like a fingerprint, it is unduplicated on any other book. However, a book may have more than one number assigned to it; for example, an Australian edition of a book first published in the United States will be given its own separate number—even if it's published by the same publisher.
4. The fourth and final number is the "check number," which makes sure the other numbers are all correct (see "The Universal Product Code," page 48, for explanation).

The Dewey Decimal System

Until 1876, books in most libraries were shelved according to subject, where they were alphabetized by author. However, as more and more books were published on a greater variety of subjects, that system was no longer efficient.

Enter librarian Melvil Dewey (1851–1931), who created a system—still in use today—that classifies books into ten broad categories, each of which has a number range:

DEWEY NUMBERS	CATEGORIES
000–099	General Works
100–199	Philosophy
200–299	Religion and Mythology
300–399	Social Sciences (including government, folklore, and customs)
400–499	Language (including dictionaries)
500–599	Pure Science
600–699	Technology
700–799	Arts
800–899	Literature
900–999	History (and geography, travel)

The advantage of Dewey's system is that the categories are able to be divided further, into subcategories. For example, under Pure Science, you'll find Mathematics (510), Astronomy (520), Physics (530), Chemistry (540), Geology (550), Paleontology (560), Life Sciences (570), Botany (580), and Zoology (590). And if you're looking for Geometry, you'll find it in the 513s. To identify even more specific categories, decimal points come into play. Finally if there are several books on the same subject, they're arranged alphabetically, by the author's last name.

Library of Congress Classifications

Because the Library of Congress must identify *every* book issued in the United States, it uses a much more detailed system than the Dewey. Subjects are broken into twenty groupings, each of which is assigned a letter. These categories are narrowed further by the addition of a second letter—for example, the broad category of Science can be divided into physics, chemistry, and so forth—and then by adding a number from 1 to 9999, which breaks the subcategories down even further. The general groupings are as follows:

A: General works
B: Philosophy and religion
C: History—auxiliary science
D: History and topography (international, not U.S.)
E and **F:** U.S. History
G: Geography, anthropology, folklore, recreation
H: Social sciences
J: Political sciences
K: U.S. law
L: Education
M: Music
N: Fine arts
P: Language and literature
Q: Science
R: Medicine
S: Agriculture, plus plants and animals as industry
T: Technology
U: Military science
V: Naval science
Z: Bibliography and library science

Note that the Library of Congress system avoids using letters that can easily be mistaken for numbers (I, O), or for other letters (W for V; X for Y).

The Elements of Drama

So much for the business of books. Now let's have a look at what's inside.

Though it's likely that prehistoric peoples acted out dramatic vignettes in their caves, full-fledged drama didn't arise until the early days of Western civilization. Greek religious ceremonies—specifically, worship of the Greek god of wine Dionysus—gave rise to comedies and tragedies. These plays were performed during festivals in Dionysus's honor and awards were given for the best of each type. A laurel wreath was given to the author of the best comedy, a goat to the writer of the best tragedy. (Try handing *those* out on national TV today!)

These stories, and later medieval dramas, standardized the form most theatrical and written presentations take.

The sequence of events in a modern drama or comedy is generally thus:

INTRODUCTION: The characters and pre-existing situation are put forth.

RISING ACTION (a.k.a. *COMPLICATION*): The conflict begins, changing the status quo.

CLIMAX (a.k.a. *CRISIS*): The conflict comes to a head.

DENOUEMENT (a.k.a. *FALLING ACTION*): The problem put forth in the plot is resolved, and any hidden information is revealed.

CATASTROPHE (In a Comedy: **RESOLUTION**): The main characters suffer their punishments or enjoy their rewards.

Poetic Meter

If you didn't have a clue as to what poetic meter was about when you were in high school, get out that old Shakespeare omnibus and follow along. Here's your chance to nail it down.

Meter is the measure of the rhythm of a line of verse, each line of which is composed of sections known as *feet*.

Lines come in different lengths, of which the most frequently used are as follows:

NAME	NUMBER OF FEET
Monometer	One
Dimeter	Two
Trimeter	Three
Tetrameter	Four
Pentameter	Five
Hexameter	Six
Heptameter	Seven
Octameter	Eight

However, there's more to poetry than just the number of feet in a line. Each foot itself can have a different length, based on the number and sound of syllables in it:

NAME	NUMBER OF SYLLABLES
Iamb	2 (one short, followed by one long)
Trochee	2 (one long, one short)
Spondee	2 (both long)
Dactyl	3 (one long, two short)
Anapest	3 (two short, one long)

At last you can figure out just what iambic pentameter truly is!

The Seven Ages of Man

Before you put that Shakespeare book back on the shelf, have a look at his play *As You Like It*. First performed in 1599, it's one of his most delightful works, and it contains one of his most famous and brilliant passages, which describes the "seven ages" of man.

With an apology to the Bard for the italics—

All the world's a stage,
And all the men and women merely players;
They have their exits and entrances;
And one man in his time plays many parts,
His acts being seven ages. At first the *infant*,
Mewling and puking in the nurse's arms. And
Then the whining *schoolboy*, with his satchel,
And shining morning face, creeping like snail
Unwillingly to school. And then the *lover*,
Sighing like furnace, with a woeful ballad
Made to his mistress' eyebrow. Then a *soldier*,
Full of strange oaths, and bearded like the pard,
Jealous in honour, sudden and quick in quarrel,
Seeking the bubble reputation
Even in the cannon's mouth. And then the *justice*,
In fair round belly with good capon lin'd,
With eyes severe, and beard of formal cut,
Full of wise saws and modern instances;
And so he plays his part. The *sixth age* shifts
Into the lean and slipper'd pantaloon,
With spectacles on nose and pouch on side,
His youthful hose well sav'd a world too wide
For his shrunk shank; and his big manly voice
Turning again towards childish treble, pipes
And whistles in his sound. Last scene of all,
That ends this strange eventful history,

Is *second childishness*, and mere oblivion,
Sans teeth, sans eyes, sans taste, sans everything.

And to answer a question you've probably wondered about for ages, a "pard" is a leopard. Ah, the confusion Shakespeare hath created simply for the sake of meter!

Dante's Levels of Hell

What comes after that which Shakespeare calls "oblivion"? For the answer to that, we turn to the Florentine poet Dante Alighieri (1265–1321).

In his *Divine Comedy*, Dante and the Roman poet Virgil take a trip to the innermost reaches of Hell. Dante's Inferno is divided into succeedingly grimmer levels:

1. **PORTAL:** The entranceway, emblazoned with the immortal phrase, "All hope abandon, ye who enter here."
2. **ACHERON:** A "woeful" river that separates our world from the underworld.
3. **CIRCLE 1 (LIMBO):** Home of the unbaptized.
4. **CIRCLE 2 (NO NAME):** Home of the "carnal sinners."
5. **CIRCLE 3 (NO NAME):** Home of the gluttonous.
6. **CIRCLE 4 (NO NAME):** Home of the prodigal and avaricious.
7. **CIRCLE 5 (STYX, MEANING ''FILTHY WATERS''):** Home of the wrathful.
8. **DIS:** The vast, walled city that contains the remainder of Hell.
   a. *Circle 6* (no name): Heretics abide here.
   b. *Circle 7:* There are three progressively lower inner circles:
      i. Phlegethon: Home of those who were violent toward their neighbors.
      ii. Home of those who were violent toward themselves.
      iii. Home of those who committed violence against God and nature.
   c. *Abyss*
   d. *Circle 8* (Malebolge): There are ten progressively deeper "bastions" in this region:
      i. *Bolgia:* Panderers, seducers.
      ii. No name: Flatterers.
      iii. No name: Simoniacs.

      iv. No name: Fortunetellers.

      v. No name: Grafters (a region of boiling, "tenacious pitch").

      vi. No name: Hypocrites.

     vii. No name: Robbers.

    viii. No name: Evil counselors.

      ix. No name: Sowers of scandal.

      x. No name: Liars.

e. *Circle 9* (Cocytus): A frozen lake.

      i. Pit of Giants.

     ii. Traitors: Divided into four inner and increasingly lower regions:

        a. Traitors to family.

        b. Traitors to country.

        c. Traitors to guests.

        d. Traitors to employers or masters.

f. *The home of "Hell's monarch," Lucifer.*

Utopian Society

Sir Thomas More (1478–1535) lost his head because he refused to acknowledge the supremacy of the English king over all other rulers.

More was no less idealistic in his writings, the most famous of which is *Utopia* (1516), a two-part chronicle. Book One presents More's view of what was wrong with the England of his time; Book Two portrays More's vision of life in an ideal country, Utopia, located on an island off the eastern coast of South America.

The political breakdown of More's Utopia is as follows:

1. **HOUSEHOLD:** These are the basic units of Utopia. Households are organized into groups of thirty.
2. **STYWARD:** Also known as a District Controller, this individual represents thirty households, and is elected for a one-year term. There are two hundred Stywards in each town.
3. **BENCHEATER:** The Senior District Controller, elected by the Stywards once a year.
4. **MAYOR:** Also elected by the Stywards from a pool of four candidates, nominated from each town's four quarters.
5. **LIETALK REPRESENTATIVE:** Each town sends three representatives to the national lietalk (parliament).

The social structure in Utopia holds that the husband is the head of the household, followed by the wife, then the children. The young are always subservient to the elders.

The hierarchy then descends to students, laborers, and slaves, the latter of which fall into three progressively lower groupings:

1. Free people from other countries who would rather serve in Utopia than live in squalor elsewhere.
2. Condemned prisoners who have been brought in from other nations.

3. Native-born Utopians. They get the worst treatment of all, since they squandered all that Utopia had to offer them.

Reflecting a rather cynical side, More named his country Utopia from the Greek *ou,* meaning "not," and *topos,* meaning "place." In other words, no place.

Brave New World

More often than not, fictional societies are not as idyllic as that of Thomas More's. In 1932, Aldous Huxley (1894–1963) wrote *Brave New World*, one of the great futuristic novels. The novel is set in a postwar era in which Henry Ford is revered as god, children are born in test tubes and raised in incubators, and a very distinct social order has emerged. So rigid is this order that embryo development among the lower castes is carefully retarded, making it impossible for anyone to be intellectually or physically equipped enough to rise above their caste.

Members of each order are identified by the color of their clothing; each order contains "plus" and "minus" levels as well. From the top:

1. **ALPHAS:** They wear gray and are "frightfully clever." An Alpha Double-Plus is an individual of the highest development.
2. **BETAS:** They dress in mulberry and, though bright, lack the edge of genius of an Alpha.
3. **GAMMAS:** Designated as "stupid," they all wear green. The lowest form, Gamma-Minus, can only tend machines.
4. **DELTAS:** Dressed in khaki, they perform menial labor only.
5. **EPSILON:** Garbed in black, these people, intellectually, are barely above the apes—especially when it comes to the Epsilon-Minus Semi-Morons.

The very lowest caste—although not officially considered as such, because its members aren't a part of civilization per se—is comprised of Savages, humans who live in primitive circumstances outside the cities, reproducing as in the old days, and viewed as thoroughly repulsive by all Alphas and Betas.

The world government of *Brave New World* is incredibly complex. It's a long chain that stretches from world leaders to the heads of various departments and its intent is to control all aspects of people's lives.

Nations are ruled by Resident Controllers; from their numbers, ten World Controllers are selected.

Beneath Resident Controllers are Secretaries and Second Secretaries, after which there are Governors and Deputy Governors. Superintendents, Assistant Superintendents, Deputy Assistant Superintendents, Directors, Assistant Directors, Chiefs, and Managers follow.

Huxley doesn't say where in the hierarchy his Chief Justices or Arch-Community-Songsters (comparable to Christian cardinals) fall.

The World of *1984*

Seventeen years after Huxley published *Brave New World,* George Orwell (1903–1950) wrote an even grimmer book about the future—*1984.*

In Orwell's thinly disguised diatribe against Russia and Stalin, ordinary citizens were more or less of equal, if undistinguished, rank. Power in the realm of Oceania was divided thus:

1. **BIG BROTHER:** The unquestioned, all-powerful leader.
2. **THOUGHT POLICE:** The all-seeing eyes and disciplining hands of Big Brother.
3. **THE INNER PARTY:** They form "the brain of the state." This group has six million members, and encompasses less than 2 percent of the population of Oceania.
4. **THE OUTER PARTY:** The commoners, or "the hands" of the state.
5. **THE LOW:** Also known as "proles," the slave population of the equatorial regions.

Surprisingly, anyone can rise above his position in Oceania: "The Party is not concerned with perpetuating its blood but with perpetuating itself."

Planet of the Apes

Here's a somewhat odder society. Before it was a hit film in 1968, *Planet of the Apes* was a novel written in 1963 by Pierre Boulle, an author best known for his novel *Bridge Over the River Kwai*.

In the wonderfully allegorical *Planet of the Apes*, Earth astronaut Ulysse Merou lands on the planet Soror, where apes are the rulers and humans the inarticulate savages. Boulle's simian society has a very distinct caste system, which was aped in the film. From the most powerful physically—and, thus, politically:

1. **GORILLAS:** Meateaters who enjoy "organizing and directing," they're simple-minded but powerful because they comprise the ape military. The guards Zoram and Zanam are typical of this order.
2. **ORANGUTANS:** Diplomatic and fairly intelligent—they have incredible memories—they've managed to finagle their way into positions of authority, especially in the sciences. They are described as "pompous, solemn, pedantic."
3. **CHIMPANZEES:** Intellectually these chimps are equal to the orangutans. But because they're physically slight, they rank last on the list.

The government on Soror is a parliament composed of three chambers, one for each hirsute race.

Mother Goose

Moving from the metaphors of great literature to the frivolousness of nursery rhymes—

The character of Mother Goose was popularized by French author Charles Perrault in his anthology *Tales of Long Ago with Morals,* published in 1697. The volume was subtitled *Tales of Mother Goose,* named for the old woman who introduced each rhyme.

Some of the immortal verse involved very rigid classifications, such as this rhyme:

A WEEK OF BIRTHDAYS
    Monday's child is fair of face,
    Tuesday's child is full of grace,
    Wednesday's child is full of woe,
    Thursday's child has far to go,
    Friday's child is loving and giving,
    Saturday's child works hard for its living,
    But the child that's born on the Sabbath day
    Is bonny and blithe, and good and gay.

The Alphabet Poem

Since the alphabet definitely has a place in this book, here's as delightful a way of presenting it as any, through one of the lesser-known Mother Goose rhymes.

ALPHABET PIE

A was an apple pie

B bit it

C cut it

D dealt it

E eat it

F fought for it

G got it

H had it

I inspected it

J jumped for it

K kept it

L longed for it

M mourned for it

N nodded at it

O opened it

P peeped in it

Q quartered it

R ran for it

S stole it

T took it

U upset it

V viewed it

W wanted it

XYZ and ampersand all wished for a piece in hand.

Around the Mulberry Bush

The origins of many schoolyard dances are lost in antiquity; likewise are the words to the chants that accompany those games.

However, many of the sing-song lyrics were published for the first time in England in 1765 in *Mother Goose's Melodies*. In order to end centuries of abuse, here are the correct words to one of the most popular of these frolics, *(Here We Go Round) The Mulberry Bush*. Originally it was used to teach children the days of the week.

The basic verse goes like this:

Here we go round the mulberry bush,
The mulberry bush, the mulberry bush.
Here we go round the mulberry bush
So early in the morning.

After that, "Here we go round the mulberry bush" is replaced, in turn, by:

1. "This is the way we wash our clothes . . . so early Monday morning."
2. "This is the way we iron our clothes . . . so early Tuesday morning."
3. "This is the way we scrub the floor . . . so early Wednesday morning."
4. "This is the way we mend our clothes . . . so early Thursday morning."
5. "This is the way we sweep the floor . . . so early Friday morning."
6. "This is the way we bake the bread . . . so early Saturday morning."
7. "This is the way we go to church . . . so early Sunday morning."

If you really want to strut your stuff next time you're out at the playground, here's the scoop on that other childhood chestnut, *Looby Loo*. The correct order for putting things in, taking them out, and shaking them all about is: right hand, left hand, right foot, left foot, head, and then the "whole self."

CLUBS AND ORGANIZATIONS

The Salvation Army

In 1865, William Booth was shocked to discover that London's local churches gave little charity to the homeless. Believing that the poor needed religion and a helping hand more than anyone, Booth established a "church for the unchurched," an evangelical mission that not only tended the spirits of the poor, but gave out food and clothing as well. The purpose of the church, which was dubbed the Salvation Army, was to see to the "total needs of the man."

Today, the Salvation Army has become a globe-wide organization, structured like the military. The branches of the Salvation Army are:

International Headquarters
Territorial Headquarters
Divisional Headquarters
Corps Command

The divisions are set up, wherever required, to meet the needs of the local population. The officers who run the operation are:

General (there's just one, and he or she is the international leader)
Commissioner (forty-five around the world, each of them a territorial commander)

Colonel
Lieutenant Colonel
Major
Captain
Lieutenant

There are just two noncommissioned ranks:

Corps Sergeant Major (responsible for meetings, schedules, etc.)
Color Sergeant (responsible for the local flags)

The Boy Scouts

The Boy Scouts were founded in England in 1907 by Robert Baden-Powell, a former soldier with a love for the outdoors. When an American, William D. Boyce, was lost in London, a scout came to his aid; Boyce was so impressed he decided to start a branch of the organization back in the States. Thus was the Boy Scouts of America founded in 1916.

The ranks of Boy Scouts are:

RANK	AGE
Tiger Cub	5–6
Cub Scout	8–10
Boy Scout	11–13
Explorer	14–21

In addition, members of the first two ranks can earn badges for their meritorious deeds. From lowest to highest, these grades are:

CUB SCOUTS
Bobcat
Wolf
Bear
Webelos
Arrow of Light
Arrowpoint

BOY SCOUTS
Tenderfoot
Second Class
First Class
Star
Life
Eagle Award
Eagle Palm

The Boy Scouts of Canada have more and slightly different ranks from that of America:

Beavers
Wolf Cubs
Boy Scouts
Venturers
Rovers

The grades for these Canadian rankings are the same, save for the Tenderfoot, Second Class, and First Class, which are Pioneers, Voyageurs, and Pathfinder Scouts, respectively.

The Girl Scouts

When Robert Baden-Powell founded scouting in 1907, it was for boys only. It wasn't long before girls asked for a group of their own, and Baden-Powell's sister and wife got the ball rolling the following year with Girl Guides. The Girl Guides soon went international and, in 1912, Juliette Gordon Low opened a Girl Guides chapter in America. It later changed its name to the Girl Scouts of the United States of America.

Girl Scouting is divided into levels, which are determined by age and/or school grade; it depends upon the tradition of the local troop.

LEVEL	AGE	SCHOOL GRADE
Daisy	4–5	Kindergarten
Brownie	6–8	1–3
Junior	9–11	4–6
Cadette	12–14	7–9
Senior	14–17	9–12

(Note: the overlap at age 14 is due to the relative sophistication of many girls at that age, and their ability to mingle effectively with the older girls.)

The Camp Fire Girls

Obviously, the early 1900s was a great time to be a kid!

In 1909, Dr. Luther Halsey Gulick and his wife Charlotte Vetter Gulick founded a girls' camp, which grew into the Camp Fire Girls, a nationwide organization devoted to "Wohelo": work, health, and love.

Today, the levels of Camp Fire Girls groupings are:

LEVEL	AGE RANGE
Bumblebee Club	4–5
Blue Bird Club	6
Adventure Club	7–9
Discovery Club	10–12
Horizon Club	13 and over

COMMERCE
AND MONEY

Dollar Denominations

For the one or two of you who may never have seen a $100,000 bill, here's what you'll find on it and on the rest of U.S. paper currency.

DENOMINATION	FRONT	BACK
$1	George Washington	Great Seal of the United States
$2	Thomas Jefferson	Signing of the Declaration of Independence
$5	Abraham Lincoln	Lincoln Memorial
$10	Alexander Hamilton	U.S. Treasury
$20	Andrew Jackson	White House
$50	Ulysses S. Grant	Capitol Building
$100	Benjamin Franklin	Independence Hall
$500	William McKinley	Denominational Design
$1,000	Grover Cleveland	Denominational Design
$5,000	James Madison	Denominational Design
$10,000	Salmon Chase	Denominational Design
$100,000	Woodrow Wilson	Denominational Design

Sadly, you can't just walk into a convenience store and ask them to break a Cleveland or a Madison. The government no longer issues bills higher than $100, though a few remain in the hands of collectors. Speaking of whom—

Coin Designations

While most of us are busy spending money, some people are collecting it. Coin collectors use the following designations to describe the condition (hence, value) of coins:

1. **P O O R :** Usually can't be identified; features badly worn.
2. **F A I R :** Information can barely be read.
3. **G O O D :** Worn, but design and printing can be identified.
4. **V E R Y   G O O D :** The design and words are legible, though portions are worn down.
5. **F I N E :** A few signs of wear on edges and design, but nothing significant.
6. **V E R Y   F I N E :** Scant signs of wear.
7. **E X T R A   F I N E :** Nearly perfect.
8. **U N C I R C U L A T E D :** Mint condition.
9. **P R O O F :** Uncirculated; mirror-like gleam.

Karatage

In the James Bond adventure *Goldfinger*, Auric Goldfinger coated a young woman's body with gold. Truth is, that's about all you can do with the stuff in its purest form: gold is simply too soft to be used for jewelry. In order to create a workable substance it has to be mixed with other metals.

Karat (or carat, when it comes to precious stones) derives from the Greek, meaning "fruit of the carob tree," the seeds of which were used by gem sellers to balance their scales. Today, the term applies to the percentage of gold vs. the percentage of an alloy.

KARATAGE	CONTENT OF FINE GOLD
24k	100%
22k	91.75%
18k	75%
14k	58.5%
12k	50.25%
10k	42%
9k	37.8%
8k	33.75%

Note: 9k and 8k are not considered legal gold karatage in the U.S. For an item even to be considered "gold plated"—that is, signifying gold that has been electroplated to another metal—the gold must be *at least* 10k, and a minimum of seven-millionths of an inch thick.

Savings Bonds

Speaking of Bond . . . savings bonds, that is . . . the country's most popular wedding and bar mitzvah gift is available in the following denominations:

DENOMINATION	PORTRAIT
$25	George Washington
$50	Franklin Roosevelt
$75	Harry Truman
$100	Dwight Eisenhower
$200	John Kennedy
$500	Woodrow Wilson
$1,000	Theodore Roosevelt
$5,000	William McKinley
$10,000	Grover Cleveland

Check Digits

Fewer and fewer Americans are using cash in their daily transactions: charge cards and checks are replacing lettuce in the economic salad.

If you're like most average Americans, you write six checks a week. But do you know what all the numbers on a check mean? Although you probably know which one is your account number (you *do*, don't you?), this is what the rest of them stand for.

First, the numbers on top (usually on the top right).

1. The first group of numerals on the left is the bank's American Banking Association number.
2. The second is your bank's individual ID number.
3. The third (below or to the right of the slash) indicates the appropriate Federal Reserve District.

On to the bottom, from the left:

1. **and 2.** These are repeats of 2 and 3 from above.
3. This is the "check number," used to make sure all the other information is correct (see "Universal Product Code" page 48, for explanation).
4. The next bunch of numbers (usually composed of four numerals) identifies your bank branch.
5. Your account number is next.
6. Finally, the number of the check is repeated.

If your check has been cashed, the amount will be printed on the right.

CRIME AND JURISPRUDENCE

International Law

Though the many infractions make the notion of international law seem laughable at times, there *is* such a thing. It pertains to matters as diverse as the rights of vessels on international waters to the sovereignty of national borders, and is created and adjudicated by the International Court of Justice, better known as the World Court. Established in 1921 in The Hague, which is located in the Netherlands, the World Court is now an arm of the United Nations.

According to the World Court, six sources must be consulted before an international law can be enacted (the court is not obliged to honor national laws, which can be prejudicial). Listed in diminishing order of importance, these sources are:

1. Treaties between nations.
2. International custom.
3. Existing national laws.
4. Previous international decisions.
5. Previous national decisions.
6. Testimony of experts from a variety of nations on international relations.

National Law

Thanks to the fundamental decency of Americans (and an occasional nudge from those folks in blue), laws work better in the United States than they do on the international scene.

Article VI of the Constitution provides the clear order of the laws of the United States. Ranked from the highest to the lowest, these are:

1. The United States Constitution
2. United States laws and treaties (all are equal in rank; the one in effect is the one that was made most recently)
3. State constitutions
4. State laws
5. Local laws (county, township, city, town, and then village)

The Federal Bureau
of Investigation

When a federal law is broken (as opposed to a state or local law), tracking down the wrong-doer is the job of the Federal Bureau of Investigation.

The F.B.I. was founded in 1908 as a minor division of the Department of Justice. It grew in size and influence a decade later, after the Communists seized power in Russia and officials feared that Reds were infiltrating the United States.

Today, the F.B.I. is headquartered in Washington, with fifty-six field offices. The hierarchy in Washington is as follows:

DIRECTOR
DEPUTY DIRECTOR
ASSOCIATE DEPUTY DIRECTORS:
  Administration
  Investigation
ASSISTANT DIRECTORS:
  Records Management
  Identification Division
  Administration Services
  Technical Services
  Training
  Intelligence
  Criminal Investigative Division
  Laboratory Division
SECTION CHIEFS
UNIT CHIEFS
SUPERVISORY SPECIAL AGENTS

In the field offices, the chain of command is:

SPECIAL AGENT IN CHARGE
ASSISTANT SPECIAL AGENT IN CHARGE

SUPERVISORY SPECIAL AGENTS
SPECIAL AGENTS

The only exception is New York City, where an Assistant Director and a Deputy Assistant top the field office roster.

Thanks to the F.B.I.'s Office of Public Affairs for their assistance in compiling this list.

The Central Intelligence Agency

The Central Intelligence Agency was founded in 1947 under the National Security Act, and was an outgrowth of the O.S.S. (Office of Strategic Services), an intelligence-gathering service founded during World War II.

The leadership of the C.I.A. is broken down as follows:

Director of Central Intelligence
Deputy Director of Central Intelligence
Executive Director
Deputy Directors (There are four: Operations, Science and Technology, Intelligence, and Administration. They are responsible for a total of twenty-four different offices, ranging from European Analysis to Photographic Interpretation Center to Training.)

In addition, the following groups and heads which have equal authority answer directly to the Director of Central Intelligence:

Director Intelligence Community Staff
National Intelligence Council
General Counsel
Inspector General
Office of Legislative Liaison

Answering to the Executive Director are four offices:

Public Affairs
Equal Employment Opportunity
Personnel
Comptroller

The Mafia

It's like the old joke: What do you call a member of the Mafia? Answer: Sir.

Founded in Sicily in the thirteenth century, the Mafia is frequently described as a lawless organization (an oxymoron, that!), and while this may be true as far as laws of the land are concerned, the criminal group actually is run according to a strict internal law of order.

The five principal ranks within the Mafia are:

1. **DON** (a.k.a. *CAPO DI TUTTI CAPI*): The boss, the head of the family.
2. **BOUGATA**: The underboss or street boss, the second-in-command.
3. **CONSIGLIORE**: A counselor, a family boss's "chief of staff," so to speak.
4. **CAPOREGIME**: The captain or lieutenant of a unit within the family.
5. **SOLDIER**: Anyone inducted into the Mafia as part of a unit (known as a *regime)*, who does the hands-on jobs of the family.

Motorcycle Clubs

Though many of their members may seem disheveled, motorcycle clubs like Hell's Angels are run according to a strict political setup. The officers of the typical gang are:

NATIONAL LEADERSHIP
President
Vice President
Secretary
Treasurer
Sergeant-at-Arms

CHAPTER LEADERSHIP (usually statewide)
Chapter President
Secretary
Treasurer

CLUB LEADERSHIP (community-wide)
Vice President
Club Counselor (usually an attorney)
Sergeant-at-Arms
Warlord
Road Captain
Patch-Wearing Members
Probationary Members
Non-Members
Ole Ladies [sic]

EDUCATION

College Degrees

Whatever your major, the four basic degrees bestowed by colleges and universities are:

DEGREE	WHAT IT MEANS
ASSOCIATE	2 years of college completed
BACHELOR'S	4 years of college completed
MASTER'S	1 or 2 years of advanced study
DOCTOR'S	2 or 3 years beyond Master's

There are two different types of doctorates: professional, for practice in certain professions (usually medical) and research, indicating mastery of a particular field of knowledge.

Schools also grant honorary degrees to people who have made exceptional contributions to a given field. Such awards are also bestowed on celebrities by schools craving publicity.

Honorary Titles

If you manage to graduate with above-average grades, you'll be recognized with an honorary title, which usually appears in Latin on the diploma itself. In order of increasing importance:

Cum laude ("with praise")
Magna cum laude ("with great praise")
Summa cum laude ("with highest praise")

FOOD AND BEVERAGE

Kitchen Measurements

If you still have trouble converting pints to quarts, tablespoons to cups, or the ever-in-demand pecks to bushels, here's a guide to liquid kitchen measurements. Some of these terms date back to Colonial America—such as the mouthful—and are not widely used these days (one can understand why), but they're valid measurements nonetheless.

10 drops	=	1 dash
2 dashes	=	1 coffee spoon
2 coffee spoons	=	1 dessert spoon
2 dessert spoons	=	1 teaspoon
3 teaspoons	=	1 tablespoon
2 tablespoons	=	1 fluid ounce
2 tablespoons (also: 2 mouthfuls)	=	1 jigger
2 jiggers	=	1 jack
2 jacks	=	1 jill
2 jills (also: 16 tablespoons)	=	1 cup
10 tablespoons	=	1 gill
2 cups	=	1 pint (i.e., 16 fluid ounces)
2 pints	=	1 quart
2 quarts	=	1 pottle
2 pottles	=	1 gallon
2 gallons	=	1 peck

2 pecks	=	1 pail
4 pecks	=	1 bushel
2 bushels	=	1 strike
2 strikes	=	1 coomb
2 coombs	=	1 cask
8 bushels	=	1 quarter (or a bulk barrel)

Oven Settings

If you're not sure what setting to use when a recipe calls for a "slow" or a "hot" oven, here's a rundown of the proper temperatures in degrees Fahrenheit (F).

DESCRIPTION	TEMPERATURE
Very cool	240
Cool	280
Slow	325
Moderate	360
Moderately hot	400
Hot	425
Very hot	465
Broil	500

U.S.D.A. Classifications

As with any bureaucracy, the U.S. Department of Agriculture doesn't exactly make things clear when it comes to grading food; what's top-of-the-line for fish is just average for eggs. The terms used for classifying food are:

FOOD	RATING (from the best)
Beef, veal, lamb	Prime
	Choice
	Good
Poultry	Grade A
	Grade B
Fish	Grade A
	Grade B
	Grade C
Pork	Acceptable
	Unacceptable
Eggs and butter	Grade AA
	Grade A
	Grade B
Fresh fruit and vegetables	U.S. Fancy
	U.S. No. 1
	U.S. No. 2

The Universal Product Code

*M*_{*ad*} Magazine once speculated that it was a joke for computers, but to most of us, the Universal Product Code is just a bunch of thick and thin lines with numbers on top. However, to the scanner at your local grocery, department, or book store, the code is a wealth of information:

1. The first numeral describes the product. Everything begins with a 0, except for variable weight items, such as vegetables and beef (2), drugs or health-care goods (3), bulk-discounted goods (4), and coupons (5). (There's no 1, because it might be misread as a bar.)
2. The five numerals that follow describe the product's manufacturer.
3. The next five numerals describe the product itself, in terms of weight, color, and other distinguishing features.
4. The last numeral is the "check number." If there is a misreading of or misprint in the preceding numbers, this number will alert the scanner. (How? The previous numbers, when added, multiplied, and subtracted a certain way, *must* total this number. If not, there's been a mistake.)

Thanks to Mike Schneider, publisher of the Haymarket Group, for serving as "check number" to the above.

The Inebriometer

At the turn of the century, an enterprising marketer—whose name is lost to us—published a chart in which the levels of drunkenness were graded. It appeared on tavern walls, more as a joke (which it was intended to be) than as a serious guide.

There's nothing at all amusing about drunkenness, but the Inebriometer is worth citing as an historical relic.

TERM	GRADE
Temperate	10
All right	5
Steady	0
Has taken a horn	− 5
Tight	− 10
Tightly slight [*sic*]	− 15
Corned	− 20
Half-seas over	− 25
Drunk	− 30
Jolly drunk	− 35
Can lie on the ground without holding on to it	− 40
Can't lie on the ground without holding on to it	− 45
Dead drunk	− 50

Alcoholic Measurements

You can refer to alcoholic beverages in pints or quarts, but you can *really* impress your friends by using these measurements for the following beverages:

BEER

Nip	=	¼ pint
Small	=	½ pint
Large	=	1 pint
Flagon	=	1 quart
Pin	=	4½ gallons
Anker	=	10 gallons
Tun	=	216 gallons

CHAMPAGNE

2 bottles	=	1 magnum
1.6 magnums	=	1 Jeroboam
3 magnums	=	1 Rehoboam
4 magnums	=	1 Methuselah
6 magnums	=	1 Salmanazar
8 magnums	=	1 Balthazar
10 magnums	=	1 Nebuchadnezzar

WINE

Tot	=	¼ gill
Noggin	=	1 gill
Bottle	=	1⅓ pints

SPIRITS

Pony	=	.5 jigger
Shot	=	.66 jigger
Jigger	=	.0935 pints
Pint	=	.625 fifth
Fifth	=	.8 quart

All of these give "holding your liquor" a new meaning, for even if you could *drink* a Nebuchadnezzar, could you *lift* one? See "Kitchen Measurements," page 44, for a more detailed explanation of jigger and gill.

Alcoholic Servings

When serving alcoholic beverages, these are the glasses to use, along with the capacity of each:

TYPE OF GLASS	CAPACITY (in ounces)
Shot glass	1–2
Pony glass	1–2
Sherry glass	3
Cocktail glass	3–6
Champagne glass	4–6
Whiskey Sour glass	5–6
Old Fashioned glass (a.k.a. Rocks glass)	8–10
Highball glass	8–10
Beer glass	10–12
Wine glass	10–14
Balloon glass	10–14
Collins glass (a.k.a. Chimney glass)	10–14
Tall Collins glass	14–16
Double Old Fashioned glass	14–16
Brandy snifter	4–48

FOREIGN HISTORY

Egypt's Pyramid

In the early days of the Egyptian civilization—in other words, from the dawn of the First Dynasty until the end of the Fourth (3100–2480 B.C.)—the pharaohs ran a more or less "hands-on" government. They personally oversaw all matters relating to their kingdom. However, as the empire grew, they were forced to delegate authority, and a great bureaucracy evolved. By the time of the Fifth and Sixth dynasties, there were over two thousand separate titles for those who served as administrators! Here are the major ones:

1. **PHARAOH:** The king of Egypt and the incarnation of the all-important sun-god Ra.
2. **CROWN PRINCE:** Heir to the throne.
3. **PRINCES:** Younger or adopted children.
4. **SUPERINTENDENT OF ALL THE WORKS OF THE KING:** Specially exalted lieutenant, responsible for recording, organizing, and carrying out the pharaoh's edicts.
5. **VIZIERS:** Any of the philosophers, sages, or scholars who advised the pharaoh. There was no set number; they were named at the whim of the ruler.
6. **KEEPERS** (a.k.a. **DIRECTORS**): Aides to the viziers.

7. **PRIESTS:** The pharoah was the arbiter of morality. Thus, the job of the priests was to oversee education, archives, science, workshops, granaries, and rites, including the all-important mummification.

8. **NOMARCHS:** Provincial rulers, equivalent to European lords.

9. **GENERAL OF THE BRAVES OF THE KING:** Leader of the boldest of the soldiers.

10. **GENERALS AND CAPTAINS:** Leaders of axemen, spearmen, archers, suppliers, reserves, etc.

11. **GRANDEES:** The noblemen who were friends and confidantes of members of the royal household. Those who were permitted to kiss the feet of the pharaoh (literally) were honored indeed.

12. **STEWARD OF THE HAREM:** The man responsible for the comfort and fidelity of the pharaoh's wives.

13. **OVERSEERS:** Those responsible for specific duties in the pharaoh's household or civic projects throughout the kingdom.

14. **SCRIBES AND ARTISTS:** The record keepers and chroniclers of the lives of pharaohs, priests, and noblemen.

The Process of Mummification

When the pharaohs or other high-ranking Egyptian officials died, it was time for mummification, a complex process that involved more than simply swathing the dead in bandages and placing them in ornate coffins. The proper preserving of remains took seventy days and involved two supervisors—a surgeon and a priest—and their assistants. The steps were as follows:

1. The embalmers erected a tent outside the house of the dead. They set up a table inside and put the body upon it.
2. The corpse was washed with water from the Nile.
3. The left side was cut open with a flint knife, and every organ was removed, save for the heart. That would be needed for weighing by the god Osiris, to determine the virtue of the deceased and, thus, his place of honor or strife in the afterlife. The removed organs were placed in urns known as canopic jars. Great Egyptians, like Tutankhamen, received an additional honor: their organs were individually bandaged and placed in miniature coffins before securing them in the urns.
4. The eviscerated body was washed on the *inside* with palm wine.
5. The brain was removed by breaking the nose and, through the use of a hooked instrument, pulling it out through the nostrils. Cedar oil was used to wash out any remnants of brain, and the skull was then filled with resin.
6. The body was covered with natron (a mixture of sodium carbonate and sodium bicarbonate), which dried and preserved the body—much like salt cures bacon.
7. The body sat, thus, for two months, during which time prayers were uttered to guarantee safe passage to eternal life in the afterworld.
8. When the actual preservation began, the body, beginning with its extremities, was wrapped in fine linen. Since the flesh would have shrunk after sixty days in the heat and natron, the swathing was padded with linen so the limbs would resemble more closely their original shape.

9. More prayers were said during this process, and oils such as olive oil and cedar oil were applied as aromatics.
10. Various charms and amulets were placed upon the mummified body.
11. The body was swathed in shrouds—four around the body and three from head to foot—which completely covered it.
12. A final prayer was uttered by the high priest, after which the funerary mask was placed on its head and the body placed in its coffin.

The Roman Army

Unlike the Egyptians, the Romans didn't mummify their leaders. In fact, the Romans had a somewhat more practical view of power. Though they revered their emperor like a god, it was an accolade they granted with a wink; everyone knew the emperor was nothing without his loyal legions and officials.

In the field, fighting men were organized as follows:

CENTURY: A force of one hundred men.

MANIPLE: Two centuries (eliminated early in the history of the empire).

COHORT: Six centuries.

LEGION: Ten cohorts.

ARMY: Two or more legions.

The officers and soldiers comprising the armies were:

IMPERATOR (a.k.a. GENERAL): Leader of an army.

LEGATE: An aide to the general.

TRIBUNE: Commander of a legion.

CENTURION: Leader of a century. Centurions were divided into *junior* and *senior* grades, and were appointed from the ranks of fighting men.

CONTUBERNALIS: A cadet who could become any rank but a centurion.

AQUILIFER: Bearer of the image of the eagle, a symbol of Rome. This honor was accorded to the finest soldier in the legion.

IMAGINFER: Bearer of the staff topped by the emperor's image.

SIGNIFER: Standard-bearer (the emblem of the army; different from the previous two symbols).

LEGIONARY (a.k.a. TROOPER): The common infantryman or cavalryman.

SAGITTARII: Archer; these men didn't truly get into the thick of things like their sword-wielding or mounted colleagues.

CORNICEN: Trumpeter.

AUXILIARIES: Equivalent to modern-day reservists.

CALONES: Servants who tended camp for the army; non-combatants.

Incidentally, gladiators did not fight in the army but only in the circuses, for the purpose of entertainment. Deserters who weren't killed were usually consigned to become gladiators. All of them were owned by wealthy Romans.

Among private citizens, the caste system revolved around five classes. Romans who owned the most property and had the greatest income belonged to the First Class, and so it went down to the Fifth. Beneath these classes was the *capite censi* (a.k.a. *proletarri*), a citizen who was free, but poor and not permitted to vote. A slave could become a freedman of this caste.

Knights were honorary titles given to men of wealth, although early in the empire's history these men were bona fide soldiers, highly regarded cavalrymen.

In any of the above-mentioned categories of private citizens, the titles *dominus* and *domina*—lord and lady—were used solely as terms of respect with no "rank," per se.

By the way, if an officer had a leave in Rome, he probably headed for a bathhouse, where he was able to take a dip in three increasingly warmer tubs:

FRIGIDARIUM (cold)
TEPIDARIUM (warm)
CALIDARIUM (hot)

Roman Rule

Support from public officials was also important to a Roman emperor. In Rome, authority was delegated as follows:

CENSOR: The highest-ranking magistrate, his duties revolved largely around the senate. A magistrate, in the Roman sense, was one who served in the executive branch of the government.

CONSUL: Lower-ranking magistrate. Fundamentally synonymous with proconsul, a consul whose term was over but who still had unfinished business to attend to. A *consul suffectus* was a temporary consul named to replace a consul who had died.

PRAETOR: Judge. There were two kinds: a *praetor urbanus,* who worked in Rome, and a *praetor peregrinus,* who practiced law abroad.

QUAESTOR: Treasurer.

SENATOR: Representative of the people. Though plebeians as well as patricians were able to become senators, the "commoners" were not allowed to speak (if allowed to speak at all) until the aristocrats had done so. (Note: rising from senator to quaestor to praetor to consul was known as the *cursus honorum,* "the path of honor.")

PREFECT: Leader of a *decury,* a group of ten *lictors.*

LICTOR: A civil servant.

In allied lands, the *client-king* either freely (or not-so-freely!) gave his full allegiance to Caesar. In conquered lands, the Rome-appointed consul (a.k.a. governor) was absolute ruler.

Worship of the gods was a serious business to the Romans, and a *pontifex* (priest) was highly regarded. The most important of these priests were the *flamines* (singular: *flamen*), who served the most revered of the Roman gods. The most honored *flamen* was the *flamen Dialis,* the priest of Jupiter. However, he was outranked by the *pontifex maximus*—the priest who served as liaison with the government.

Viking Caste

Meanwhile, up in the frigid north, the history of the Vikings goes back roughly twelve thousand years, when the Ice Age glaciers retreated and hearty folk settled in what is now Scandinavia. The early history of the Norse is that of a warring, exploring people who lived in districts ruled by local kings. However, sometime around A.D. 900, Harald Fairhair conquered vast regions of Norway and instituted an organized system of government.

He divided his realm into *fylkir* (shires), and then established a hierarchy from the king on down:

HIRDMEN: The king's personal bodyguards. During times of war, they were his military leaders; in peace, they saw to it that the fylkir were run according to his laws.

CHIEFTAIN: Leader of a flyki.

JARL: The official who oversaw tax collecting. Comparable to a European earl.

HERSIR (plural: **HERSAR**): An agent who did the jarl's bidding.

BONDI: Literally, "household owners." They were primarily farmers, fishermen, and traders—though the group included all people who were allowed to own property, livestock, or boats.

LEYSINGI: Freedmen who were former *thralls*. They were not *free*men, per se, because they were free only so long as they worked for the owner who had freed them. However, they did possess legal and political rights.

THRALLS (SLAVES): Primarily foreign captives or debtors.

Chinese Sages

There have been fifteen Chinese dynasties since prehistory (which ended circa 1100 B.C.). In all, the emperor was the unquestioned ruler, with dukes and generals considered beneath him.

The hierarchy of Chinese government really was not much different from that of England's or other feudal systems'—but what *was* unique was the high regard the Chinese had for a "sage." The term described one who excelled in any discipline, though the Chinese (up through the Manchu Dynasty, which ended in 1912) respected their sages in the following order, from the most-honored:

1. Science
2. Medicine
3. Astrology
4. Politics
5. Physical fitness
6. Military skill
7. Sports
8. Music
9. Military strategy

The steps to achieving sage-dom were these:

1. Possessing the correct values and discipline.
2. Applying those values and discipline to action.
3. Causing the action to produce results.
4. Using the results to reinforce values and discipline.

The Chinese even respected—though did not condone—sages of thievery. One scribe went so far as to rank the qualities that made a robber a sage:

1. Wisdom ("They know what is possible and what is not")
2. Intelligence ("To know where peoples' treasures are hidden")
3. Bravery ("To enter, without hesitation, peoples' homes")
4. Propriety ("After leaving a home, they do not act suspiciously")
5. Fairness ("They divide the booty fairly")

Confucian Philosophy

His name—before Anglicization—was Kung Fu-tzu, and he was not a martial artist but a master teacher. Confucius lived in China from 551–479 B.C. and taught students poetry, courtesy, and music, which he felt were the three cornerstones of "a person's character." He was also the author of the Golden Rule: "Do not do to others what you would not have them do to you."

At the base of Confucius's philosophy were "the steps to a sane and orderly world." These were:

1. People should strive to be honest, courageous, and courteous.
2. So doing, they can run their family with wisdom and love.
3. If a family is respectful and moral, the government they choose will be ethical.
4. If the leaders are wise and just, the environment will breed personal honesty, courage, and courtesy—thus completing a successful circle.

Brilliant but a trifle testy, Confucius took his disciples and went into exile when the ruler of his home state of Lu ignored his advice.

The Chinese Calendar

Before leaving ancient China, a look at the calendar reveals that, although the philosophers, priests, and teachers may have had their heads (if not their bodies) in the clouds, the farmers had their feet firmly planted on the soil.

An agricultural society, China divided its year into twenty-four months. Moreover, these months were not named for gods, as in the Gregorian calendar, but for what happened during that particular fortnight.

MONTH	MEANING	GREGORIAN DATES
Li Chun	Spring Begins	2/5–2/19
Yu Shui	Rain Water	2/20–3/5
Jing Zhe	Excited Insects	3/6–3/20
Chun Fen	Vernal Equinox	3/21–4/4
Qing Ming	Clear and Bright	4/5–4/19
Gu Yu	Grain Rains	4/20–5/5
Li Xia	Summer Begins	5/6–5/20
Xiao Man	Grain Fills	5/21–6/4
Mang Zhong	Grain in Ear	6/5–6/20
Xia Zhi	Summer Solstice	6/21–7/7
Xiao Shu	Slight Heat	7/8–7/22
Da Shu	Great Heat	7/23–8/7
Li Qui	Autumn Begins	8/8–8/23
Chu Shu	Limit of Heat	8/24–9/7
Bai Lu	White Dew	9/8–9/23
Qui Fen	Autumn Equinox	9/24–10/8
Han Lu	Cold Dew	10/9–10/22
Shuang Jiang	Frost Descends	10/23–11/7
Li Dong	Winter Begins	11/8–11/22
Xiao Xue	Little Snow	11/23–12/6
Da Xue	Heavy Snow	12/7–12/22
Dong Zhi	Winter Solstice	12/23–1/6
Xiao Han	Little Cold	1/7–1/21
Da Han	Severe Cold	1/22–2/4

Celtic Society

Unlike the Massachusetts basketball team, the name of these primitive Europeans is pronounced with a hard *c*. Like the NBA Celtics, though, the European Celts were winners: While the Vikings were busy to the north, the Celts, who were a synthesis of many different regions, dominated much of what is now England, France, Switzerland, Germany, and other Baltic and Mediterranean regions for hundreds of years. They reached the height of their power in 500 B.C., after which they were conquered piecemeal over the next two centuries and brought under Roman rule.

Celtic society was a loosely knit organization of farming settlements grouped into villages. Within each village, the hierarchy was as follows:

1. **CHIEFTAIN:** One headed each village. In many places, they were elected at annual meetings from the ranks of nobles or warriors.

2. **DRUIDS:** Wise men and judges who also supervised religious rites.

3. **NOBLES:** Major landowners and merchants.

4. **WARRIORS:** Cavalrymen and charioteers who were regarded most highly in the days in which the Celts' rule began to wane; even the Romans dreaded their fierce charges.

5. **METAL-WORKING SMITHS:** Without their craft, the arts of war and farming would have suffered. And since gold was the coin of the realm, the ability to work it into handy chains or bars proved quite useful.

6. **BARDS:** Though the Druids were the keepers of local histories, the Bards interpreted and applied it, a skill much admired by the Celts.

7. **FREE PEASANTS:** Small landowners.

8. **SEMI-FREE PEASANTS:** Laborers bound to a noble but free to have possessions.

9. **RETAINERS:** Servants who lived with the nobles; they were one step above slaves.

10. **SLAVES:** Very few of these remained a part of the population for most were sold or used in blood sacrifices. These were primarily men taken prisoner in battle.

Feudal England

If you were living in England circa 1130, toward the end of the reign of Henry I—son of William the Conqueror—you would have found England a far more structured and civilized place than when the Celts and Romans ruled.

Henry the First put a system of government into place that satisfied his former rival kings by giving them generous land grants (a.k.a. "fiefs"). Thus did he turn them into his allies.

The status of Englishmen in the twelfth century was as followeth:

KING: Also known as the *lord* or *overlord*, there was no questioning his will. (Unless you were the testy Oliver Cromwell five centuries later, who helped to lop a king's head off.)

VASSALS: Many noblemen who were former kings. They submitted to the king's will in exchange for vast holdings and relative autonomy therein. These men were also known as *feudal lords*.

KNIGHTS: Then as now, honored members of the court—but without the political clout of a lord.

STEWARDS: Men who managed secondary manors (that is, those other than the one of the feudal lord) which were a part of the fief. Stewards were sometimes appointed from among the knights.

PRIESTS: Though Henry II would diminish their influence considerably, they—along with monks and nuns—were more or less left alone by the lords. In addition to ministering to their flock, they worked church lands and fed the poor.

SCHOLARS: Teachers in church-run schools who were highly regarded. Then as now, many also held other jobs.

TOWNSMEN: The merchants and craftsmen who kept the local economy humming. Although they were free, they had very little disposable income.

SERVANTS: Some were free, while others were merely elevated serfs. Few outside of the nobility and wealthy merchants had servants.

SERFS: The peasants who worked the land for the lords. Though technically not slaves, they weren't free to change jobs or leave the manor without their lord's approval.

The Steps to Knighthood

The feudal period in English history is probably best remembered by most of us for its knights. And although we tend to think of Camelot when we think of knights—those glorious, chivalrous men in gleaming silver armor—the truth of the breed is somewhat less romantic. Knights actually were highly paid professional fighting men who were chivalrous for purely practical reasons. For them, kindness and mercy to friend and foe was often done in the spirit of self-preservation, as a knight who was victorious one day might be a loser the next, and today's enemy might be tomorrow's friend. Only toward the end of the Middle Ages, when the church pressed knights to set examples for the community, did a purer form of chivalry emerge.

Theoretically, anyone could rise to become a knight, and the process was this:

1. **PAGE:** At the age of seven, a boy could be sent to live with a knight willing to take him on. This not only gave the youth experience in the ways of being a knight, it got him away from any pampering his mother might be inclined to give. Pages were taught to ride and use weapons, and had menial chores to perform around the manor.

2. **SQUIRE:** When the page reached the age of fourteen, he became the knight's "shield bearer." In addition to waiting tables and cleaning for the household, it was his job to see that the knight's arms were clean and in good repair. He also took serious training in weaponry, acquiring armor of his own and learning how to move, fight, and even *leap* into a saddle while fully dressed and armed.

3. **KNIGHT:** A successful squire was named a knight by the knight under whom he'd trained. If his parents had the money, he became a landed lord in his own right. If not, he became a mercenary. Frequently, unlanded squires were not permitted to ascend to knighthood.

Knighthood ended circa 1500 with the coming of foot soldiers equipped with firearms. Not even fifty-five pounds of armor and mail could stop a bullet! The title of "Knight" then became purely honorary, with modern-day English knights using the title "sir" and a woman who is knighted using the title "dame."

Marks of Cadency

Throughout all of Europe in the Middle Ages, marks of cadency were added to the family's basic coat of arms when a knight had children. These designs signified "differencing"; that is, the order of birth for sons. (Unfairly, daughters received only a nondescript, diamond-shaped "lozenge.")

The practice—which continues on in many families today—employs these designs:

ORDER OF BIRTH	ADDITION TO COAT OF ARMS
Eldest	Label (resembling a downward-pointing "E" on an eyechart; often superimposed over the family arms)
Second	Crescent with cusps pointing upwards
Third	Mullet (a five-pointed star)
Fourth	A swallow
Fifth	A ring
Sixth	A fleur-de-lis
Seventh	Five hearts in a rose atop a mullet
Eighth	A cross

English Titles

After you've been knighted, where is there to go in the English hierarchy? Quite a way, if you're fortunate enough to inherit a peerage, marry into one, or have one created for you by the crown. From the lowest titles:

COMMONERS	ADDRESSED AS
1. Lord or Lady	(Nothing)
2. Knight or Dame	Sir or Dame
3. Baronet or Baronetess	Sir or Lady

NOBLES	
4. Life Baron or Life Baroness	My lord or my lady
5. Baron or Baroness	My lord or my lady
6. Viscount or Viscountess	My lord or my lady
7. Earl or Countess	My lord or my lady
8. Marquess or Marchioness	My lord or my lady
9. (Nonroyal) Duke or Duchess	Your grace

ROYALS	
10. Prince or Princess	Your royal highness
11. Duke or Duchess	Your royal highness
12. King or Queen	Your majesty

The English earl is the equivalent of a count, the preferred title in some European countries. The title "dowager" is used by widows of peers, while "lady" is employed primarily in one of three ways: as an informal alternative to any woman's title, save duchess; as a title of respect for untitled members of noble families, such as wives of younger sons; and to honor the wives of knights.

The Japanese Hierarchy

A strict "caste" system dominates Japanese culture today and it derives from a centuries-long tradition of classes. That tradition was so rigidly upheld that, until early in this century, members were unable to escape their designated class.

In Japan, the emperor was the unquestioned leader, the god-on-earth. Below him were eleven classes, in descending order of importance:

Princes
Noblemen
Priests
Military Officers
Soldiers (Samurai)
The Educated (doctors, teachers, scientists)
Farmers
Merchants
Commoners (craftspeople, peasants, servants, seamen)
Beggars
Christians

Although this type of hierarchy no longer prevails in modern-day Japan, others do exist—especially when it comes to the corporate culture. So, if you're thinking of doing business in Japan, it would be best to learn the following chain of command. In this case the ranking officer isn't necessarily the chief "hancho"!

1. Kaicho: Chairman
2. Shacho: President
3. Fuku Shacko: Vice-President
4. Bucho: Department Manager
5. Kacho: Section Manager
6. Kakiricho: Supervisor
7. Hancho: Foreman

India's Caste System

Like the Japanese, the Indians of Asia have a strict caste system. It originated about 1500 B.C., when Aryans invading from the northwest grouped people in neighborhoods according to the jobs they held. The system ossified and survives to this day. Neither wealth nor education will permit a person to rise above her or his caste. From highest to lowest, then:

1. **BRAHMANS:** Priests
2. **KSHATRIYAS:** Members of the royal or warrior castes
3. **VAISYAS:** Merchants or professional people
4. **SUDRAS:** Workers

Beneath these are the so-called untouchables, the beggars and/or diseased. Though the caste system was officially banished by their constitution, it is still, unofficially, a part of Indian life.

The Six Types of Government

The United States is unique in that it has had only one form of government since its inception. This is not the case with most other nations.

Though there have been refinements over the years—not all of them good ones—these are the six basic forms of government, ranked from control by the fewest to control by the most:

ANARCHY: Rule by no one

AUTOCRACY (a.k.a. **MONARCHY**): Rule by one leader

OLIGARCHY (a.k.a. **ARISTOCRACY**): Rule by a few leaders

PLUTOCRACY: Rule by the wealthy

OCHLOCRACY: Rule by a mob

DEMOCRACY (a.k.a. **POLITY**): Rule by all the people

GAMES

Chess Values

A game of chess frequently involves the swapping of pieces: If I take your knight, you take my rook. But is that really a wise trade?

Chess players generally have a rule of thumb to follow when faced with just such a decision, one which assigns numerical values to the pieces. And these are, from the most powerful to the least:

PIECE	WORTH
Queen	9
Rook	5
Bishop	3.5
Knight	3.5
Pawn	1

The king isn't assigned a value since it can never be swapped. Once your king is taken—that's it. The game is *finis*!

Now, if you're confused about whether you qualify as a chess master or an expert, this'll clear it up for you. A variable number of points is assigned to each particular match, the winner adding them to her/his score, the loser subtracting them.

From lowest ranking to highest:

TITLE	POINT VALUE
Class C	Under 1600
Class B	1600–1799

TITLE	POINT VALUE
Class A	1800–1999
Expert (a.k.a. Candidate Master)	2000–2199
Master (a.k.a. National Master)	2200–2399
Senior Master (a.k.a. International Master)	2400–2599
Grandmaster	2600 and over

Anyone interested in learning more about the intricacies of chess should contact the United States Chess Federation.

Bridge Points

Like chess, the game of bridge is strictly ranked. Titles in tournament play are awarded according to how many points a competitor has. As players win in club, unit, sectional, regional, and North American play, they earn points of increasing value:

1. **RATING POINT:** The building blocks of the scoring system.
2. **MASTER POINT:** Equivalent to 100 rating points, this is awarded in club games.
3. **BLACK POINT:** Same as a master point, but awarded for competition beyond the club level, in sectional and regional play.
4. **RED POINT:** A master point won in national and North American competition.
5. **GOLD POINT:** A master point given for national victories.

As the points increase, titles are awarded thus:

TITLE	POINTS REQUIRED
Sub-Master	Under 100 rating points
Junior Master	1–19 masters
Master	20–49 masters
National Master	50–99 masters
Senior Master	100–199 master points
Advanced Senior Master	200–299 master points, 20 or more of which must be red or gold
Life Master	300 master points or more, 50 or more of which must be red or gold

Thanks to bridge maven Roy Erickson for sharing his knowledge of the game.

Poker Hands

Got a yen for poker? Better have a *lot* of yen, since the chances of being dealt a winning hand are up there with the probability of being hit by a meteorite. Each hand consists of a combination of cards; a hand comprised of a ten, jack, queen, king, ace, in the same suit is better (and obviously more difficult to get) than a pair of threes! Here are the winning poker hands that are possible, from the one guaranteed to get you the game, to the one least likely to get you that win.

HAND	POSSIBLE COMBINATIONS IN ANY GIVEN DECK	ODDS OF GETTING ONE
Royal Flush	4	649,739:1
Straight Flush	36	72,192:1
Four of a Kind	624	4,164:1
Full House	3,744	693:1
Flush	5,108	508:1
Straight	10,200	254:1
Three of a Kind	54,912	46:1
Two Pairs	123,552	20:1
One Pair	1,098,240	1.37:1

Another way of looking at the odds is decimally; while your chances of being dealt a pair is .42, the likelihood of getting *any* kind of straight flush is .00002.

The different number of hands that can be dealt in poker is 2,598,960. So when you're dealt hand number 2,598,961, don't be surprised if déjà vu sets in!

Darts Scoring

Darts originated in English taverns, with the original projectiles being daggers flung at the bottoms of wine casks.

Today, the dart board is broken into twenty segments shaped like long pie pieces, each of which meets at a bull's-eye. Upon striking a triangle, the player is awarded the number of points listed beside that triangle (the range is between one and twenty points). Here are the points earned for hitting various other sections:

SECTION	POINTS
Yellow bull's-eye	50
Black ring around the bull's-eye	25
Middle ring	The points for the triangle it intersects are tripled.
Outer ring	The points for the triangle it intersects are doubled.

Nintendo Rankings

It started as a guide to proficiency for the Nintendo Entertainment System videogame *Faxandau,* and quickly spread throughout Nintendodom as a gauge for excellence.

Here are the titles bestowed upon videogame players, in diminishing order of importance, along with the percentage of a given game-mission they must conquer to earn that title.

RANK	PERCENTAGE
Lord	100
Paladin	92–99
Superhero	85–91
Champion	78–84
Myrmidon	71–77
Soldier	64–70
Hero	57–63
Warrior	50–56
Veteran	43–49
Chevalier	36–42
Adept	28–35
Fighter	21–27
Battler	14–20
Aspirant	7–13
Novice	0–6

Hangman Segments

We've all played *Hangman*, the game where an opponent picks a secret word, we call out a letter, and for every time our letter does not appear in that word our adversary draws another part of the gallows . . . then starts hanging a human body from it. When the drawing of the body is finally complete, it means we've lost—and our opponent has won.

Unfortunately, some people try to stave off defeat by cheating. They force the artist to add to the body facial features, fingers, toes, a navel, and so forth. According to the rules of the original game, which originated in England in the last century, that isn't permitted. The order and absolute limit of drawn segments is:

1. Ground
2. Gallows upright
3. Gallows horizontal beam
4. Gallows diagonal support beam
5. Noose
6. Head
7. Body
8. Right arm
9. Left arm
10. Right leg
11. Left leg

That's it, folks!

Scrabble Scoring

S crabble was invented in 1931 by unemployed architect Alfred M. Butts. An average of one million sets are sold worldwide each year—a good argument indeed for quitting your job and hitting the worktable.

The popularity of the game derives not just from the challenge of spelling words with the letters at hand, but from skewering your opponent by placing a high-point word on a triple-word-score space.

The point values and distribution of letters were determined by Butts through trial-and-error play with a prototype of the game. He finally settled upon the following. From the letters least likely to push your score over the top, to the letters with the highest values:

LETTER	POINT VALUE
Blank	0
A, E, I, L, N, O, R, S, T, U	1
D, G	2
B, C, M, P	3
F, H, V, W, Y	4
K	5
J, X	8
Q, Z	10

The distribution of letters breaks down as follows:

LETTER	NUMBER IN SET
A	9
B	2
C	2
D	4
E	12
F	2
G	3

LETTER	NUMBER IN SET
H	2
I	9
J	1
K	1
L	4
M	2
N	6
O	8
P	2
Q	1
R	6
S	4
T	6
U	4
V	2
W	2
X	1
Y	2
Z	1
Blank	2

On the board itself, players will find increased point-value squares as follows:

SQUARES	NUMBER ON BOARD
Double letter	24
Triple letter	12
Double word	17
Triple word	8

Using all seven letters on your rack in one word earns you an additional fifty points.

Billiard Balls

Beginning in the fourteenth century, the French played a form of
billiards—known as "lawn bowling"—outdoors, on the grass. Louis
XIV finally brought it inside, putting it on a table in the late seventeenth
century—presumably on a rainy day when he wanted to play. (The
English also take credit for having done this; however, since "billiards"
derives from the Old French word "billart," for "playing stick," we'll
give the nod to Louis.)

Today, billiards—also known as "pocket billiards"—is played with
sixteen different balls, which are colored as follows:

BALL	COLOR
Cue	White
1	Yellow
2	Blue
3	Red
4	Purple
5	Orange
6	Green
7	Deep Red
8	Black
9	White with a yellow stripe
10	White with a blue stripe
11	White with a red stripe
12	White with a purple stripe
13	White with an orange stripe
14	White with a green stripe
15	White with a deep red stripe

The term "pool" originated in the 1880s, when betting on horse races
was done in a "pool-room"—so-called because of the pool-betting that
went on there (i.e., a means of controlling the odds by betting heavily on
certain horses). While men waited for results of the races, they played
billiards. Eventually, the games they played, from Eight Ball to Progression, took on the colloquial name.

GEOGRAPHY

Waterways

It's interesting the way certain bodies of water have become attached to descriptive phrases. Why is it called a *stream* of consciousness, and not a river? Why did desert sheiks describe themselves as *rivers* to their people, not brooks?

The descriptions are actually quite appropriate. A river of consciousness implies something mightier than meandering thoughts, while rivers carry cargo, an image that suited the sheiks who brought food and riches to their tribes.

To help you create metaphors of your own, here's how the running waters stack up:

1. **RIVER:** A large body of water flowing in a definite course, usually terminating in a sea, gulf, or bay. There are three kinds: *consequent,* which flows down a slope; *subsequent,* a tributary; and *obsequent,* a tributary of a subsequent river.
2. **STREAM:** A body of water flowing through a channel or flowing only seasonally.
3. **BROOK:** A small, freshwater stream. If the small stream is not freshwater, it's called a *rivulet.*
4. **CREEK:** A stream that's smaller than a brook or rivulet.

Bodies of Water

Compared to defining flowing waters, categorizing still bodies of water is a piece of lake . . . err, cake! Though the difference between a gulf and a bay is a tough call, the rest are fairly well defined:

1. **O C E A N :** Any distinct section of the vast body of salt water that covers our world. An ocean must stretch at least between two continents.
2. **S E A :** A large body of water that is marked off on two or three sides—usually of a single continent—by land. Seas are sometimes subdivisions of oceans.
3. **L A K E :** A large body of water completely enclosed by land.
4. **G U L F :** A large body of water that extends into the land.
5. **B A Y :** An arm of an ocean or lake that extends into the land, but is considerably smaller than a gulf.
6. **I N L E T :** A narrow passage, usually between islands.
7. **F J O R D :** A narrow inlet situated between cliffs or high banks.
8. **S T R A I T :** A narrow stretch of water connecting two larger bodies.
9. **L A G O O N :** Shallow water partly or entirely separated from a larger body.
10. **P O N D :** A landlocked body of water too small to be a lake, and often artificially created. If the waters are still, a pond is referred to as a *pool*.
11. **P U D D L E :** A small pool.

Latitudes

We can remember left from right, up from down, inside from outside—so why are longitude and latitude so tough? Maybe it's because longitude measures distances east and west of Greenwich, England, yet the lines run north and south. Some of us are *that* easily confused. Besides, *long*itude sounds like it should be a line going from left to right, not up and down.

Be that as it may, latitudes are arranged in groups depending upon where they fall. The three headings are:

LATITUDE	LOCATION
High	Between sixty degrees and the South or North Pole. Sixty degrees south is located below the tip of South America; in the north, it nearly bisects Anchorage, Alaska.
Middle	Those latitudes between the high and low latitudes.
Low	Latitudes that extend thirty degrees north and south of the equator. In the south, that's the tip of Africa; in the north, New Orleans, Louisiana.

Sailors have also referred to a region known as the "horse latitudes," a.k.a. the doldrums. These areas are approximately thirty degrees north and south of the equator at the fringes of the trade wind belt. The waters here are calm, the winds gentle, and so the ships move slowly. Some believe the term derives from the fact that horses died during slow transit through the region. More likely, though, the phrase is rooted in the complaints of sailors who were paid in advance and received no overtime when they plied slowly through the region (i.e., they were working off a dead horse).

Biological Land Regions

Once scientists had broken down life forms as far as they could go, you'd think they'd be satisfied (see "Biology Classes," page 1). 'Fraid not. It occurred to zoologists late in the last century that animals should be categorized by their geographical occurrence as well. Thus, they came up with five "regions," which are, from the largest to the smallest:

NAME	REGION	REPRESENTATIVE LIFE
Holarctic	North America, Mexico, Europe, North Africa, Asia north of the Himalayas	Bear, rabbit, moose, timber wolf
Ethiopian	Most of Africa and the Middle East	Zebras, gorillas and chimpanzees, giraffes, lions, African elephants
Neotropical	Central and South America	Monkeys with tails, anteaters, sloths, guinea pigs
Oriental	India, Southern China, parts of Malaysia and Indonesia	Tigers, Indian elephants, orangutans
Australian	Australia, New Guinea, New Zealand	Kangaroos, koalas

GEOLOGY

Planetary Layers

Try this on for size, Atlas: Our world weighs 5,879,000,000,000,000,-000,000 tons (look *that* one up in the *Mathematical Systems* section), and iron appears to be the most abundant element. The Earth consists of an atmosphere (the blanket of air that surrounds the world), a hydrosphere (its water), and a lithosphere (the planet's crust).

Here's how the latter breaks down, from the earth beneath our feet to the bowels of the planet. (Note: the distances are approximate.)

LAYER	AVERAGE DEPTH FROM SURFACE
Crust	Ranges from 5 miles deep (minimum) to 50 miles (maximum)
Upper Mantle	1745 miles
Asthenosphere	1980 miles
Lower Mantle	2100 miles
Liquid outer core	2800 miles
Transition region	2900 miles
Solid inner core	3000 to 5000 miles

To give you an idea how far down we *haven't* gone digging into the Earth's surface, the Soviet Union's Ministry of Geology—which manages a thirty-story-tall drilling derrick for subterranean research—has established three different kinds of holes, defined by their depth. Despite their lofty names, these holes have—literally!—only scratched the surface:

1. Deep Hole, from four to seven kilometers deep
2. Superdeep Hole, from seven to ten kilometers deep
3. Ultradeep Hole, eleven miles deep and beyond

Atmospheric Divisions

If we turn our eyes from the center of the Earth to its outer reaches, we'll find these divisions for the air blanket that surrounds our world. From the surface, which touches Earth, to the fringes of outer space:

TROPOSPHERE: Extends 10 miles from the surface (the outside boundary of it being known as the *tropopause*)
STRATOSPHERE: 10–30 miles (location of the ozone layer)
MESOSPHERE: 30–55 miles
THERMOSPHERE (a.k.a. **HETEROSPHERE**): 55–435 miles
EXOSPHERE: 435–600 miles

The one region of the atmosphere that overlaps the others is the *Ionosphere*, which reaches 30–250 miles. It's a region in which the air is ionized (i.e., electrified), due to pummeling from ultraviolet radiation and X rays from the sun. It consists of the following divisions, which affect the reflection and, thus, the transmission of radio waves:

D Region: 35–55 miles
E Region (Heaviside-Kennelly Layer): 55–95 miles
F Region (Appleton Layer): 95–250 miles

Land Masses

Sure, you memorized the seven continents in the third grade. But did you also learn their area? And the percentage of the Earth's land they represent? If not, here's your chance.

There'll be a test later.

CONTINENT	SQUARE MILES	PERCENTAGE OF LAND
Asia	17,128,500	29.5
Africa	11,707,000	20.2
North America	9,363,000	16.2
South America	6,875,000	11.8
Antarctica	5,500,000	9.5
Europe	4,057,000	7.0
Australia	2,966,136	5.1

The remaining 0.7 percent of Earth's land consists of islands and the like.

Crustal Rifts

These terms describe openings in the Earth's surface. They aren't defined by feet or meters, but by their relative size and other attributes. From the largest to the smallest:

1. **CANYON:** A very deep valley, often with a river or stream running through it.
2. **GORGE:** A narrow canyon, usually with steep walls.
3. **DALE:** A broad valley.
4. **RAVINE:** A deep valley.
5. **VALLEY (or VALE):** A depression between mountains or areas of raised land. Also known as a *col*.
6. **GLEN:** A narrow valley.
7. **DELL:** A smaller valley, usually wooded.
8. **DINGLE:** A narrow dell.
9. **HOLLOW:** A very small valley. Also called a *notch*.
10. **FISSURE:** A narrow opening created by the movement of land masses, usually during an earthquake.
11. **GULLY:** A deep trench.
12. **TRENCH:** A long hole, usually worn into the ground by running water.

If we were to include attributes of other worlds as well, the largest opening of all would be a *rille*, which is a long, deep canyon.

Mountain Ranges

Unlike canyons, gorges, and the like, Earth's mountains don't fall into size categories. There are hills, there are mountains—and that's it! (Check the dictionary definition for hill; most likely, it'll say, "An elevation smaller than a mountain." Not terribly illuminating.)

However, every mountain *is* broken down into sections. Their demarcation varies, depending on the size and location of the mountain (a tropical mountain will obviously have a different alpine zone than a polar one), but the order remains the same across all. From the bottom up:

BASE: The lowest point from which a perfectly horizontal plane can be measured.

FOOTHILLS: The low hills that are attached to the base of a mountain, but are not a part of the main peak(s). These are divided into:

Low-altitude Foothills
Middle-altitude Foothills
High-altitude Foothills

Trees and/or plants grow in foothills.

ALPINE ZONE: Begins where the tree-line ends, though hardy mosses and other flora may exist in this region.

PEAK: An area not found on older mountains that have suffered eons of erosion; here, the mountain narrows considerably and near-vertical ascent is the only way to scale it successfully.

SUMMIT: The very top of the mountain.

Layers of Soil

Moving from the gargantuan to the minuscule, we come to soil, which is a blend of organic and inorganic matter. Plunge a spade into the soil, and the layers you'll encounter are:

TOPSOIL: Consists of humus (decaying organic matter), minerals, and water.
SUBSOIL: Primarily composed of minerals and water, with limited amounts of humus.
SOIL MATERIAL: Small pieces of rock from below, and water from above.
ROCK: The raw material for the *soil material* level.

The *topsoil* and *subsoil* levels can range from a few inches to a few feet deep, depending upon the climate, amount of decay, use or disuse of the region for farming, and so forth.

Sand Widths

Regardless of how it may look to the untrained eye, not all sand (which is mostly ground-up quartz) and sand-like material is the same. These are the different kinds of grains and their sizes:

GRAIN TYPE	DIAMETER (in inches)
Clay	.00008 and under
Silt	.00008–.002
Sand	.002–.08
Granule	.08–.15
Loam	A mixture of all the above

Getting into the higher-sized rocks, we find:

Pebble	.15–.25
Pea gravel	.25–.50
Bank-run gravel	.50–3.0
Cobble (a.k.a. cobblestone; cob, when referring to coal)	3.0–10.0
Boulder	10 and over

Earthquake Scales

Most people have heard about the earthquake scale created in 1935 by Charles F. Richter of the California Institute of Technology. It describes the real magnitude of earthquakes *logarithmically*—that is, each whole number increase represents a tenfold increase in the force of the quake.

While this is a valuable tool for seismologists, the Mercalli Scale is much more useful for ordinary people caught in a quake. Devised by Giuseppe Mercalli in 1902, this scale more accurately describes what someone on the surface actually *feels*.

The outer limits of the Mercalli Scale are roughly equivalent to 3 and 8.5 on the Richter Scale.

RICHTER NUMBER	CHANGE IN MAGNITUDE
1	1
2	10
3	100
4	1,000
5	10,000
6	100,000
7	1,000,000
8	10,000,000

MERCALLI NUMBER	CHARACTERISTICS
I	Detectable only by seismic instruments.
II	Barely noticeable on the surface; hanging plants may swing.
III	Minor disturbance, equivalent to a passing truck; most likely to be felt by people in tall buildings.
IV	Dishes will rattle, walls will groan, and cars will rock. More like a freight train passing nearby than a truck!

V	Strong enough to rouse someone from sleep. Windows may break, statues may topple.
VI	People will experience difficulty in standing; trees will sway, furniture may slide, walls may crack.
VII	Streets will split; there may be light damage, such as chimneys collapsing.
VIII	Structures may be seriously compromised; smokestacks and old walls may be destroyed, furniture overturned.
IX	Buildings will collapse or be thrown off foundations; minor fissures.
X	Metal will bend; even sturdy structures will fall. Wide fissures.
XI	Massive destruction, landslides, tidal waves; bridges will collapse.
XII	Absolute destruction, landscape radically changed. Objects not only toppled but flung about.

If you're curious about just how powerful an earthquake measuring 8 on the Richter Scale would be, consider this. An erg is the metric unit equal to the amount of energy it takes to move one gram a distance of one centimeter in one second. A magnitude 8 earthquake would release *600 quintillion* ergs. The largest earthquake ever recorded, in Japan in 1923, released even more—a staggering *twenty sextillion* ergs.

There's one more system the U.S. Department of the Interior, Geological Survey, uses to measure earthquakes: A level alert. Comprised of Levels C–A, it indicates the chances of a shock occurring within the next twenty-four hours, with Level A being the most likely.

HEALTH AND MEDICINE

Stages of Anesthesia

Prior to the first use of anesthetics in surgery, patients were given alcohol, drugs such as mandrake and opium (which either weren't powerful enough to work, or too powerful and killed them), or simply tied down or held. In most cases, surgery was limited to just a few minutes—which was really all that the patients could bear.

The first operation using anesthesia was performed by Dr. William T.G. Morton at Massachusetts General Hospital on October 16, 1846. In this instance Morton used ether, but since then, many other anesthetics have been used during surgery.

Regardless of the chemical chosen, these are the stages through which a patient passes before and during surgery. *Planes 1* and *2* are as far as it goes, if all proceeds according to plan.

STAGE I: ANALGESIA The period from the beginning of anesthetization to the onset of loss of consciousness.

STAGE II: DELIRIUM Loss of consciousness.

STAGE III: SURGICAL

Plane 1: Rhythmic respiration

Plane 2: Volume of air during respiration is usually decreased; breathing quickens or slows, depending upon the patient.

Plane 3: Muscles in the rib cage (intercostal) experience some paralysis, causing a long pause between breaths, then sudden intake.

Plane 4: Breathing may become so gasping or jerky that the surgeon is chagrined; anesthesia may have to be deepened, occasionally leading to—

STAGE IV: RESPIRATORY PARALYSIS The patient stops breathing and must be revived. Quickly.

Abnormal Growths

Here's some knowledge you'll want to flaunt at the next company picnic to ensure that raise you've been after.

Abnormal growths or elevated wounds of the skin have different names, depending upon their size and composition. From the smallest to the largest, these are:

TERM	DIAMETER (in mm)	DESCRIPTION
Vesicle	5 or less	Contains fluid, elevated
Bulla	5 or more	Solid, elevated
Nodule	5–10	Solid, can be elevated
Pustule	5–10	Contains pus
Papule	10 or less	Solid, elevated
Macule	10 or less	Flat, discolored
Tumor	20 or more	Large nodule
Plaque	20 or more	Group of papules

Another category, wheals, are transient marks of widely varying sizes.

Burns

The subject of burns wasn't much in the news until Richard Pryor and Michael Jackson ended up in burn centers for mishaps with coke and Pepsi, respectively.

Here are varying degrees of burns, with examples of their causes and a few possible treatments.

TYPE	EXAMPLE OR SYMPTOM	TREATMENT
First degree	Sunburn; steam	Medicated skin cream, heals within a week.
Second degree	Scalding, holding hot metal	Medicated cream and bandages, heals in 2–3 weeks.
Third degree	Fire	Requires a doctor's care. Since a full layer of skin is destroyed, grafting will be required.
Circumferential	Any burns (often electrical) that completely encircle a limb or body region (such as the chest), which can impair circulation or respiration	Requires a doctor's care; fasciotomy (repair of connective tissue) sometimes required.
Chemical	Acid, alkali	Wash with water initially (for up to a half hour); follow up with a doctor's care.
Electrical	Destruction of muscles, nerves, circulatory system, etc., below the skin	Give victim fluids, followed with a doctor's care and ECG monitoring.

Height and Weight Scales

The Department of Health and Human Services feels that if you're outside these boundaries (which means above and beyond your waistband), it wouldn't hurt to lose a few pounds.

Obviously, those with slighter builds will skew toward the smaller end of the scale, and vice versa.

HEIGHT	WOMEN	MEN
4'10"	92–119	
4'11"	94–122	
5'	96–125	
5'1"	99–128	
5'2"	102–131	112–141
5'3"	105–134	115–144
5'4"	108–138	118–148
5'5"	111–142	121–152
5'6"	114–146	124–156
5'7"	118–150	128–161
5'8"	122–154	132–166
5'9"	126–158	136–170
5'10"	130–163	140–173
5'11"	134–168	144–179
6'	138–173	148–184
6'1"		152–189
6'2"		156–194
6'3"		160–199
6'4"		164–204

HOLIDAYS AND CELEBRATIONS

Birthstones

An offshoot of the ancient origins of astrology (see "Astrological Signs," page 218) is the belief that certain precious and semiprecious stones and flowers are lucky for those born in certain months. Though contemporary accounts are rare, it seems clear that the peoples of China, Greece, and other ancient civilizations—perhaps inspired by the pagan earth-worshipers of prehistory—believed that minerals had the power to influence humankind.

Here, then, is the pastiche distilled from centuries of tradition:

MONTH	BIRTHSTONE	FLOWER
January	Garnet	Snowdrop
February	Amethyst	Primrose
March	Bloodstone or Aquamarine	Violet
April	Diamond	Daisy
May	Emerald	Hawthorn
June	Pearl, Alexandrite, or Moonstone	Rose
July	Ruby	Water lily
August	Peridot or Sardonyx	Poppy
September	Sapphire	Morning glory
October	Opal or Tourmaline	Hops
November	Topaz	Chrysanthemum
December	Turquoise or Zircon	Holly

Anniversary Traditions

The original idea, rooted in medieval practice, was to give couples gifts that reflected their progressive wants or achievements during married life. Paper symbolized the success of the marriage covenant, cotton (diapers) the arrival of a child, leather and linen the need for clothing, wood for household repairs and furnishings, and so on.

The tradition has carried over into the modern day as follows:

YEAR	GIFT
1	Paper
2	Cotton
3	Leather
4	Linen
5	Wood
6	Iron
7	Wool or copper
8	Bronze
9	Pottery
10	Tin or aluminum
11	Steel
12	Silk
13	Lace
14	Ivory
15	Crystal
20	China
25	Silver
30	Pearl
35	Coral or jade
40	Ruby
45	Sapphire
50	Gold
55	Emerald
60	Diamond

It's doubtful many young couples would welcome a scratch pad for their first anniversary . . . so the Jewelry Industry Council has very thoughtfully promulgated a somewhat classier (if somewhat self-serving) notion of what one should present to couples celebrating anniversaries.

1	Gold
2	Garnet
3	Crystal
4	Blue topaz
5	Small sapphire
6	Amethyst
7	Onyx
8	Tourmaline
9	Lapis
10	Diamond
11	Turquoise
12	Jade
13	Citrine
14	Opal
15	Small ruby
16	Peridot
17	A watch
18	Cat's-eye
19	Aquamarine
20	Small emerald
25	Silver jubilee
30	Pearl jubilee
35	Large emerald
40	Large ruby
45	Large sapphire
50	Golden jubilee
60	Diamond jubilee

The Twelve Days of Christmas

Whether you call it Tebet, Dhu'l-hijja, or Pansa, when December rolls around you'll be hearing a lot of this song. Yet despite how often they sing it, few people are aware of what "The Twelve Days of Christmas" really means.

The song was originally sung in England, circa 1700. Celebrating the days between Christmas and Epiphany, it's ripe with symbolism—much of which can only be speculated at today. The partridge symbolizes a loss of faith in church lore (i.e., it's the bird that leaves its young), while rounding a pear tree three times was once believed to reveal to a maiden the image of her true love. The French hens are Bretons, the four birds are collied (not *calling*), or black birds, and the five golden rings are ringed pheasants. When originally sung, the song was a game: every time a singer messed up, some kind of penance was exacted.

On each of the twelve days of Christmas, the singer's "true love gave to me," from first to last:

A partridge in a pear tree
Two turtle doves
Three French hens
Four collied birds
Five golden rings
Six geese a-laying
Seven swans a-swimming
Eight maids a-milking
Nine ladies dancing
Ten lords a-leaping
Eleven pipers piping
Twelve drummers drumming

HUMAN BIOLOGY

The Elemental Body

Anyone ever tell you you're "all wet"? Don't take it personally . . . you *are*! The human body is mostly water—with some of the fifteen following compounds and elements thrown in to keep us from being walking bottles of Evian:

COMPONENT	PERCENTAGE
Water	61.8
Protein	16.6
Fat	14.9
Nitrogen	3.3
Calcium	1.81
Phosphorous	1.19
Potassium	.24
Sodium	.17
Magnesium	.041
Iron	.0075
Zinc	.0028
Copper	.00015
Manganese	.00013
Iodine	.00004
Misc. (cobalt, molybdenum, etc.)	.19982

Fractures

A baby is born with three hundred bones, many of which fuse together as the child grows, leaving him with 206 bones as an adult. Yet many of them are prone to breakage, and the different kinds of fractures that can be sustained are, from the least severe:

FRACTURE	WHAT IT MEANS
Hairline	The bone splits in a slender line, usually lengthwise
Pathological	A break caused by disease; usually a minor fracture
Greenstick	Incomplete fracture, in which the top or bottom is fractured along its length, while the other portion remains whole
Fatigue	The bone splits, usually more than in a greenstick fracture
Depressed	The bone has been pushed inward; may be snapped
Simple (a.k.a. Closed)	The bone has snapped, but does not break the skin
Comminuted	A section of the bone has been shattered into fragments
Compound	Broken bone has pushed through the skin

Cells

In the five quarts of blood that pulse through the body of a healthy adult—they make a round trip through a sedentary person once every *minute*—the following types of cells are found, from the largest to the smallest:

TYPE OF CELL	DIAMETER (in inches)
White corpuscles (leucocytes)	.00036–.0008
Red corpuscles (erythrocytes)	.0003
Platelets (thrombocytes)	.000078

In terms of density in the blood, the order of cells is as follows:

TYPE OF CELL	NUMBER (per cubic millimeter)
Red corpuscles	5 million
Platelets	250,000
White corpuscles	5,000 to 10,000

Skin

When you give someone a "high-five," you're also giving them what might be called a "deep-five," since there are five different levels of skin:

EPIDERMIS

A covering of cells consisting of the following strata:

1. Comeum: The dead cells on top.
2. Granular: A comparatively rough level just beneath the surface.
3. Spinous: A spiny, tightly knit layer.
4. Basal: The cells that make up the base.

DERMIS

The inner layer consisting of nerve endings, sweat glands, hair follicles, and blood vessels. In other words, all the important things.

Dream Rhythms

Scientists don't know why we dream. They say the brain may be cataloguing information it picked up during the day (acting like a computer, where all the shifting around sometimes causes strange things to appear on the screen), is throwing out data it doesn't want (which may account for the often haphazard scenarios of dreams), or is creating pleasant or taxing situations to help us work through emotional distress.

Whatever the reason, dream we do, and most people who are deprived of dreams or sleep for very long suffer disorientation, an inability to concentrate, and even hallucinations.

What researchers *can* tell us about dreams is this: First, although everyone may not remember his or her dreams, all people dream, every night. Second, while scientists once believed that dreams were compressed into the space of just a few seconds, they now know that that isn't so. Dreams occur, more or less, across real time. Third, there's no connection between nightmares and foods that upset the stomach. So . . . eat that rarebit and dream pleasant dreams!

Most people fall asleep within fifteen minutes. After that, their sleep is divided into distinct stages. In eight hours of sleeping, the average person goes through three periods, which are broken down as follows:

1. **LIGHT SLEEP:** Brief periods of light sleep—often lasting for no more than fifteen minutes—which buffer the periods of deep sleep.
2. **DEEP SLEEP:** After 1½ to 2 hours, a person enters into a deep sleep.
3. **REM SLEEP:** After falling into a deep sleep, the sleeper begins dream sleep. REM stands for "rapid eye movement." During such dream periods, the dreamer's eyes move back and forth, as though following the action. (The only people who don't have REM are those who have been blind since birth.) Different people dream for different lengths of time; some dream in more or less equal periods of thirty minutes, while others start out by having a dream of from five to ten minutes, and end up with a dream lasting nearly an hour.

Taste Buds

When food or drink washes over your tongue, you don't taste it the same way on all parts of the tongue. There are four kinds of taste buds, and if your tongue were divided like a clock, here's where they'd be located:

TASTE	LOCATION
Sweet	From five to seven o'clock
Salt	From three to five o'clock, and from seven to nine o'clock
Sour	From two to three o'clock, and from nine to ten o'clock
Bitter	From eleven to one o'clock.

There are no taste buds in the regions between one and two o'clock, or ten and eleven o'clock, nor do the taste centers overlap. If you're eating Chinese food and a mouthful misses a section of your tongue, you may end up with just sweet *or* sour pork!

The Human Brain

ate in 1990, Dr. Frank Lynn Meshberger of St. John's Medical Center in Anderson, Indiana, made an interesting suggestion in the pages of *The Journal of the American Medical Association:* He claimed that Michelangelo's *Creation of Adam* on the ceiling of the Sistine Chapel is actually a painting of the human brain. The flowing robe surrounding the figure of God is, in silhouette, an exact likeness of the brain, while the leg of the angel hanging from the bottom is a ringer for the medulla. Since Adam is already alive in the painting, what God would be giving him through his outstretched finger is not life, but the mind.

Yet Michelangelo couldn't have known much about the brain's inner workings back then. And although many questions still remain, we've basically figured out what each part of the brain is responsible for. So, from the bottom up:

1. **THE BRAINSTEM:** The oldest part of the brain, having evolved over a half-billion years ago. Not surprisingly, it very much resembles the brain of a reptile and is comprised of:
   a. *Spinal Cord*
   b. *Medulla:* Controls breathing, the heart, and blood pressure.
   c. *Pons:* A band of nerve fibers.
   d. *Midbrain:* a.k.a. the *mesencephalon,* a sensory center.
2. **CEREBELLUM:** The "small brain," responsible for muscular coordination and certain kinds of memory.
3. **PITUITARY GLAND:** Regulates growth and controls other glands.
4. **HYPOTHALAMUS:** In charge of body temperature, hunger and thirst, and certain aspects of emotional behavior.
5. **HIPPOCAMPUS:** Plays a role in learning and memory.
6. **THALAMUS:** Something of a switchboard for incoming information.
7. **BASAL GANGLIA:** Composed of the *lentiform nucleus* and *caudate nucleus,* both of which help control movement.

8. **CORPUS CALLOSUM:** A bunching of nerve fibers; there are approximately 300 million of them.
9. **CEREBRUM:** Also known as the *forebrain*, it's the seat of thought and action. The Cerebrum is divided into two hemispheres, left and right.
10. **CEREBRAL CORTEX:** The surface layer, which is composed of, from the bottom up:
    a. *Temporal Lobe:* Hearing and memory.
    b. *Occipital Lobe:* Vision.
    c. *Parietal Lobe:* Language, logic.
    d. *Frontal Lobe:* Decision-making and behavior.

Keep in mind that the size of the brain has no bearing on intelligence (an elephant's brain is physically larger than ours). Rather, intelligence is dictated by the number of folds in the cortex.

The left and right sides of the brain are believed to control, respectively, logic (especially language) and creativity.

Finally, in regards to the color of the brain: We call it gray matter because the sections that do most of our heavy-duty thinking are gray. However, the cerebral cortex is pink due to the many small blood vessels winding through it, while other sections of the brain are white.

And what did Michelangelo have to say about that?

He painted the robe red.

Teeth

No one likes to think about their teeth. Most of us wouldn't even go to the dentist if we didn't get those officious little postcard reminders . . . and even *then* we put it off a month or two. Or three.

It's fascinating, though, when you realize that our teeth are arranged like a little automobile assembly line, each with its own job to perform before passing the food along.

Teeth on the bottom and top rows are distributed exactly the same. From front and center to the back of your mouth they are:

INCISORS: Eight in all, these sharp, square teeth cut the food. The front two incisors of the upper and lower jaw are *middle incisors*. One *lateral incisor* is located on either side of each pair.

CUSPIDS: Four in all, one on either side of the lateral incisors, they hold and tear the food. Also known as *canines*.

BICUSPID: Two of these follow each cuspid, and help with the rending of food. The inner-most of each pair are called *premolars*.

MOLARS: There are twelve of these grooved, flat teeth, which grind food to pulp. They come in around ages six, twelve, and eighteen. The eighteen-year molars are also known as "wisdom teeth," a term shortened from "To cut one's wisdom teeth," which happens at approximately the time a person reaches maturity. Appropriately, some people never get these teeth.

HUMAN
HISTORY

Historical Eras

The saga of life on Earth occupies roughly a third of our planet's
history . . . and the history of humans on Earth occupies an even
smaller amount of time than that. Relatively speaking, civilization as we
know it to date *must* have been an afterthought.

Earth's history is divided into eras which, along with their subdivisions, periods and epochs, have no specific length attached to them.
Rather, they demarcate landmarks in the earth's development.

Here is the history of our world (P = period, E = epoch):

ERA	YEARS AGO	CHARACTERISTICS
ARCHEOZOIC	5 billion–1.5 billion	Earth's formation to 1-celled life
PROTEROZOIC	1.5 billion–600 million	Bacteria to multicelled organisms
PALEOZOIC		
Cambrian P.	600–500 million	Marine invertebrates
Ordovician P.	500–440 million	Crustaceans, algae, seaweed
Silurian P.	440–400 million	Air-breathing animals begin to appear
Devonian P.	400–350 million	Fish and amphibians
Mississippian P.	350–300 million	Mollusks, insects, land areas

ERA	YEARS AGO	CHARACTERISTICS
Pennsylvanian P.	300–270 million	Large reptiles, swamps
Permian P.	270–220 million	Reptiles dominant
MESOZOIC		
Triassic P.	220–180 million	Volcanoes and early dinosaurs
Jurassic P.	180–135 million	Dinosaurs dominant; conifers abundant
Cretaceous P.	135–70 million	Dinosaurs become extinct; flowering plants, modern insects
CENOZOIC		
Paleogene P.		
Paleocene E.	70–60 million	Rise of birds and mammals
Eocene E.	60–40 million	Modern mammals appear
Oligocene E.	40–25 million	Heyday of saber-tooth cats
Neocene P.		
Miocene E.	25–10 million	Grazing mammals dominant
Pliocene E.	10–1 million	Direct human ancestors; mountains increase in numbers; climate cools
Quaternary P.		
Pleistocene E.	1 million–10,000	Glaciers bring on Ice Age
Holocene E.	10,000–Present	Humans dominant; rise of civilization

The Mississippian and Pennsylvanian periods are also known, collectively, as the Carboniferous Period. The Paleogene and Neocene periods are also known as the Tertiary Period.

There are also further subdivisions to all of the eras. For example, the Triassic can be broken into Scythian, Anisian, Ladinian, Karnian, Norian, and Rhaetian periods, while the Jurassic embraces the Hettangian, Sinemurian, Pliensbachian, Toarcian, Aalenian, Bajocian, Bathonian, Callovian, Oxfordian, Kimmeridigian, and Tithonian periods. These, however, are quite properly of interest only to paleontologists.

The Ice Age is itself broken down into several phases, defined as follows:

1. Lower Pleistocene, consisting of the Nebraskan glacial phase, lasting from 1 million to 450,000 years ago.
2. Middle Pleistocene, comprised of the Aftonian pluvial (interglacial) phase, the Kansanian glacial phase, the Yarmouthian pluvial phase, and the Illinoian glacial phase, lasting from 450,000 to 100,000 years ago.
3. Upper Pleistocene, made up of the Sangamonian pluvial phase, and the Early Wisconsin and Late Wisconsin glacial phases, lasting from 100,000 to 10,000 years ago.

Human Evolution

While all life derived from the first single-celled organisms that appeared some 3.8 billion years ago, the human tree can be traced directly to the hairy, arboreal, herbivorous quadruped Dryopithecus that lived about 36 million years ago.

Dryopithecus spawned three different species: the orangutan, the gorilla, and a chimpanzee-like animal. Some twenty million years ago, the latter divided into the chimpanzee and the hominids—us.

The hominid line threads through evolution as follows:

SPECIES	YEAR	DISTINCTIVE QUALITIES
Ramapithecus	15 million years ago	Chimp-sized; possible use of stones and sticks as weapons.
Australopithecus	4 million years ago	Australopithecus africans were bipedal with human-like teeth; the Paranthropus line was physically larger with smaller brains. Other lines include Australopithecus bosei (a.k.a. Zinjanthropus) and Australopithecus robustus.
Homo habilis	2 million years ago	Nearly five feet tall, with a large brain. A hunter.
Homo erectus	1.5 million years ago	One of the pithecanthropines, this hominid tamed fire and possessed a culture that included religious rites and art.

SPECIES	YEAR	DISTINCTIVE QUALITIES
Homo sapiens	100,000 years ago	Built huts and made clothing. Some 50,000 years ago, the stars of the line were the brutish but physically modern Neanderthals and the Cro-Magnons. The latter species continued to evolve; the Neanderthals became extinct.
Homo sapiens sapiens	40,000 years ago	Modern humans.

Ages of Civilization

The dawn of civilization is not marked by the taming of fire, as one might suspect, but by the coming of agriculture and therefore permanent settlements. The key events that pre- and post-dated this event are:

AGE	YEARS	EVENTS
OLD STONE AGE (a.k.a. Paleolithic P.)		
Lower Paleolithic P.	500,000–250,000 B.C.	Pebble tools, hand axes
Middle Paleolithic P.	250,000–60,000 B.C.	Flake tools
Upper Paleolithic P.	60,000–10,000 B.C.	Blade tools, the beginning of agriculture
MIDDLE STONE AGE (a.k.a. Mesolithic P.)	10,000–8000 B.C.	Microliths (small stones used for construction)
NEW STONE AGE (a.k.a. Neolithic P.)	8000–5000 B.C.	Battleaxes, advanced stone
COPPER AGE	5000–3500 B.C.	First use of copper
BRONZE AGE	3500–1000 B.C.	Copper and tin mixed to form bronze
IRON AGE	1000–4th Century B.C.	Tools made from iron

The Iron Age is generally regarded to have ended when Alexander the Great marched into India and found the natives using steel.

Greek Ages

Unlike modern archaeologists and anthropologists, the Greeks divided history into five separate ages. These periods were chronicled in the works of Hesiod and other poets. No dates are provided for those eras that are patently mythological; indeed, it would be more accurate to refer to these ages as symbolic of the evolution of Hellenic civilization, rather than as periods bounded by years.

1. **THE GOLDEN AGE:** The era before Zeus, occurring prior to recorded time, when Cronus ruled. It was an age of innocence and joy.
2. **THE SILVER AGE:** The name is a misnomer. Zeus ascended to the throne of Olympus and instituted all unpleasantness on Earth: changing seasons, death and decay, and day-to-day hardship.
3. **THE BRAZEN AGE** (circa 2000–1500 B.C.): A time of bronze (figuratively), when humans waged war with unparalleled ferocity.
4. **THE HEROIC AGE** (circa 1500–1000 B.C.): The period surrounding the Trojan War.
5. **THE IRON AGE:** An ongoing age of corruption, warfare, and misery.

LANGUAGE AND SPEECH

Indo-European Languages

L anguage is believed to have originated some 1.5 million years ago, arising either from attempts to mimic natural sounds, repeated cries of surprise or exertion, or the growth of chants associated with rites or religion. Most likely, it was a combination of all the above.

Indo-European spawned all of the languages on the following list, most of which then followed a complex evolution. For example, the roots of modern-day Spanish began with Indo-European, and went to Italic, Latin, Proto-Romance, Proto-Continental Romance, Proto-Western Romance, South Ibero-Romance and North Ibero-Romance (Portuguese and Catalan respectively), which mingled to form Spanish.

The dates indicate when the fully developed languages appeared. Afro-Asiatic and Sino-Tibetan tongues aren't included.

LANGUAGE	YEAR OF ORIGIN	WHERE SPOKEN
1. Indo-European	circa 5000 B.C.	Lithuania
2. Sanskrit	circa 2000 B.C.	India
3. Greek	circa 1800 B.C.	Greece
4. Latin	600 B.C.	Italy
5. French	A.D. 842	France
6. Spanish	A.D. 950	Spain
7. Italian	A.D. 960	Italy
8. English	A.D. 700	England
9. German	A.D. 500	Germany

Etymological Distinctions

You see these distinctions whenever you look up the etymology of a word: Old English, Middle English, and Modern English. Here's what they mean:

1. **OLD ENGLISH (A.D. 449–A.D. 1100)**: Also known as Anglo-Saxon, this form of English arose when the southern Britons, fearing invasion from the northern Picts and Scots, invited Germanic peoples from across the English Channel to settle on the island. As the Germanic tongue became predominant, the language subsequently became infused with words brought over by the Roman Catholic missionaries and Danish invaders. In A.D. 700 the language stabilized, more or less. Subsequent changes have largely been in the addition of new words, pronunciation of old ones, and the evolution of more complex grammar.

2. **MIDDLE ENGLISH (1100–1500)**: When William the Conqueror invaded England, countless French words infiltrated—and were absorbed into—the English language. For a while, French and the new hybrid English vied for dominance. English won out in 1362 when it was declared the official language of the legal system and in the schools.

3. **MODERN ENGLISH (1500–PRESENT)**: The teaching of Latin and Greek in the school system occasioned new words into the language that, not surprisingly, were of Roman or Greek origin.

The Greek, Hebrew, and Arabic Alphabets

Three of the oldest alphabets still in use today are Greek, Hebrew, and Arabic. In many cases, the names of the letters are remarkably similar across each alphabet, indicating just how much the Greeks borrowed from the older civilizations in the Middle East.

GREEK	HEBREW	ARABIC
Alpha	Aleph	Alif
Beta	Beth	Ba
Gamma	Gimel	Ta
Delta	Daleth	Tha
Epsilon	He	Jim
Zeta	Vav	Ha
Eta	Zayin	Kha
Theta	Het	Dal
Iota	Teth	Dhal
Kappa	Yod	Ra
Lambda	Kaf	Zay
Mu	Lamed	Sin
Nu	Mem	Shin
Xi	Nun	Sad
Omicron	Samekh	Dad
Pi	Ayin	Ta
Rho	Pe	Za
Sigma	Sadhe	'Ayn
Tau	Koph	Ghayn
Upsilon	Resh	Fa
Phi	Sin	Qaf
Chi	Shin	Kaf
Psi	Tav	Lam
Omega		Mim
		Nun
		Ha
		Waw
		Ya

MATHEMATICAL SYSTEMS

Roman Numerals

In the beginning, Roman numerals were simply marks: I was 1, IIIII was 5, and so on. When that proved unwieldy, the symbol "V" was devised to signify 5 (representing five spread fingers), and "X" was used to signify two "V"s. "C" was selected from the word *centum* (100), and "M" was derived from *mille* (1,000). The origins of L and D are not known.

Why the ongoing fascination with Roman numerals? Why do we continue to use them in books and carve them in cornerstones? They're classy, for one thing, but they're also practical—not likely to be confused with street numbers, and a suitable way to set off the early sections of a book (e.g., iii, ii, and i are much classier than -3, -2, and -1).

ROMAN NUMERAL	ARABIC EQUIVALENT
I	1
II	2
III	3
IV	4
V	5
VI	6
VII	7
VIII	8
IX	9

ROMAN NUMERAL	ARABIC EQUIVALENT
X	10
XI	11
XIX	19
XX	20
XXX	30
XL	40
L	50
LX	60
XC	90
C	100
CD	400
D	500
CM	900
M	1,000
$\bar{\text{C}}$	5,000
$\bar{\text{X}}$	10,000
$\bar{\text{L}}$	50,000
$\bar{\text{C}}$	100,000
$\bar{\text{D}}$	500,000
$\bar{\text{M}}$	1,000,000

Mayan Numerals

Tucked away in Central America, the Mayan numeral system never caught on the way the Roman system did. (It did among the Mayans—but they never tried to conquer Europe and spread it around.)

From roughly 1500 B.C. to A.D. 1500, the Mayans used the following numerals:

MAYAN	ARABIC EQUIVALENT
Clam shell	0
.	1
..	2
...	3
....	4
—	5
— with .	6
— with ..	7
— with ...	8
— with	9
═	10
═ with .	11
═ with ..	12
═ with ...	13
═ with	14
≡	15
≡ with .	16
≡ with ..	17
≡ with ...	18
≡ with	19

When the Mayans needed to go to 20 and beyond, they simply added new rows.

Hindu Numerals

If Roman and Mayan numbers aren't confusing enough, wait till you get a load of the numerical progressions in Hindi. For unknown reasons, there are no equivalents to several numbers in use today, such as one million.

HINDI NAME	AMERICAN EQUIVALENT
Ek	One
Das	Ten
San	Hundred
Hazar	Thousand
Lakh	Hundred thousand
Crore	Ten million
Arahb	Billion
Carahb	Hundred billion
Nie	Ten trillion
Padham	Quadrillion
Sankh	Hundred quadrillion

Arabic Numerals

E ven in our familiar Arabic numerals there are numbers that are as tongue-twisting as "crore" and "carahb" to say (see Hindu numerals, preceding page). If you ever need really big figures—to count your wealth or the number of attoseconds in a human lifetime—here are the numbers you'll be using:

NUMBER	AMOUNT OF ZEROES
1. Thousand	3
2. Million	6
3. Billion	9
4. Trillion	12
5. Quadrillion	15
6. Quintillion	18
7. Sextillion	21
8. Septillion	24
9. Octillion	27
10. Nonillion	30
11. Decillion	33
12. Undecillion	36
13. Duodecillion	39
14. Tredecillion	42
15. Quattuordecillion	45
16. Quindecillion	48
17. Sexdecillion	51
18. Septendecillion	54
19. Octodecillion	57
20. Novemdecillion	60
21. Vigintillion	63
22. Googol	100
23. Quintoquadagintillion	138
24. Centillion	303
25. Googolplex	googol

Unlike the other numbers, the term "googol" has no Latin derivation. It was coined by the young nephew of Edward Kasner, a mathematician who felt the need for such a number. The other really big numbers (i.e., those following a trillion) evolved in spurts—quadrillion and quintillion first being used in 1674, sextillion and septillion arriving in 1690, nonillion being coined in 1828, and so on. No one was using them for practical measurements, mind you—they were used in theory, nothing more.

Thanks to Ken Ogan, Ph.D., for taking time out from his isotacho-phoresis research to dust off his old MIT texts and collect this information.

The Binary System

A "bit," or a "binary digit," is the building block of computer memory, the smallest unit of computer information. Here's what you've got when you have a lot of them:

8 bits	=	1 byte
1,000 bytes	=	1 kilobyte (1K)
1,000 kilobytes	=	1 megabyte

For purposes of comparison, a Nintendo Entertainment System works with 8K of memory, while a good personal computer like the IBM PS/2 comes with 512K.

If you're wondering why the term "binary" is used at all, the answer is simple. Every computer circuit needs only two commands to function: on or off. You need only two numbers to send those instructions: 0 for off, and 1 for on. It's the many combinations of "0" and "1," of switches that are to be on or off, which allow a computer to process information.

You can pretty well figure out how the binary system works by examining the numbers from 1 to 20:

NUMBER	BINARY NUMBER
0	0
1	1
2	10
3	11 (two and one)
4	100
5	101 (four and one)
6	110 (four and two)
7	111 (four and two and one)
8	1000
9	1001
10	1010 (eight and two)
11	1011 (eight and two and one)
12	1100

NUMBER	BINARY NUMBER
13	1101
14	1110
15	1111
16	10000
17	10001
18	10010
19	10011
20	10100

Clearly, by the time you get a few thousand of these things going, you've got a lot of information flowing!

Mathematical Prefixes

Next time you curl up with a nice comforting physics text, don't make that oh-so-common (and embarrassing!) error of confusing a picosecond with a femtosecond.

Here, from biggest to smallest, are multiple or fractional prefixes and their meanings. (Hollywood producers, take note: Stop referring to big money as "megabucks"; start using "gigabucks" and "exabucks." It'll be very hip.)

PREFIX	MEANING
Exa-	Quintillionfold (i.e., multiplied by 1,000,000,000,000,000,000)
Peta-	Quadrillionfold (three zeroes less than our friend exa-)
Tera-	Trillionfold (three less, again)
Giga-	Billionfold (again, three less)
Mega-	Millionfold
Kilo-	Thousandfold
Hecto-	Hundredfold
Deka-	Tenfold
Deci-	One-tenth
Centi-	One-hundredth
Milli-	One-thousandth
Micro-	One-millionth
Nano-	One-billionth
Pico-	One-trillionth
Femto-	One-quadrillionth
Atto-	One-quintillionth

Polygons

If you're terrible at math, this is the last law of order you'll want to read. On the other hand, it'll come in handy when your kid asks, "How many faces does a dodecahedron have?"

Here are the names given to different polygons, or multisided figures:

Triangle: 3 sides
Quadrilateral: 4 sides
Pentagon: 5 sides
Hexagon: 6 sides
Heptagon: 7 sides
Octagon: 8 sides
Nonagon: 9 sides
Decagon: 10 sides
Dodecagon: 12 sides
Quindecagon: 15 sides

If you're a glutton for punishment, here are the names for different polyhedra, a polyhedron being a solid shape on which all the faces are planes:

Tetrahedron: 4 faces
Cube: 6 faces
Octahedron: 8 faces
Dodecahedron: 12 faces
Icosahedron: 20 faces

Angles

Lines that have just one end point are known as rays. When two different rays share the same end point, they form an angle.

An angle is measured by the number of degrees between its rays where they intersect an imaginary circle. (A degree is one of the 360 equal segments into which a circle is broken.)

There are four different kinds of angles:

ANGLE TYPE	DEGREES ENCOMPASSED
Acute	Up to 90 degrees
Right	Exactly 90 degrees
Obtuse	Over 90 degrees, but under 180 degrees
Straight	180 degrees

MILITARY AND ARMAMENTS

U.S. Military Ranks

Who salutes whom in the American armed forces? Here's a quick guide, from top to bottom:

COMMISSIONED OFFICERS
(Five Star) General of the Army
(Four Star) General
Lieutenant General
Major General
Brigadier General
Colonel
Lieutenant Colonel
Major
Captain
First Lieutenant
Second Lieutenant

WARRANT OFFICERS *(These officers—who rank below the above-mentioned commissioned officers—take their title from the warrant, or certificate, which grants them their authority.)*
Chief Warrant Officer, Grade Four (W-4)
Chief Warrant Officer, Grade Three (W-3)

Chief Warrant Officer, Grade Two (W-2)
Warrant Officer, Grade One (W-1)

NONCOMMISSIONED OFFICERS *(Note: the "E" designation is for Enlisted person.)*
Sergeant Major of the Army (E-9)
Command Sergeant Major (E-9)
Sergeant Major (E-9)
First Sergeant (E-8)
Master Sergeant (E-8)
Platoon Sergeant (a.k.a. Sergeant First Class) (E-7)
Staff Sergeant (E-6)
Sergeant (E-5)
Corporal (E-4)

ENLISTED MEN
Specialists (E-4) (Specialists have technical or administrative duties that entitle them to rank, but not to the exercise of command.)
Private First-Class (E-3)
Private (E-2)
Private (E-1)

The Air Force, Army National Guard, and Air National Guard follow the same system for officers. In the Air Force, enlisted personnel rank as follows, from the top down:

Chief Master Sergeant
Senior Master Sergeant
Master Sergeant
Technical Sergeant
Staff Sergeant
Sergeant
Senior Airman
Airman First Class
Airman

The Marines are ranked the same as the Army for officers and warrant officers. Enlisted personnel are graded as follows:

Sergeant Major
Master Gunnery Sergeant
First Sergeant
Master Sergeant
Gunnery Sergeant
Staff Sergeant
Sergeant
Corporal
Lance Corporal
Private First Class

The Navy and Coast Guard ranks are as follows:

OFFICERS
Fleet Admiral
Admiral
Vice Admiral
Rear Admiral (upper half)
Rear Admiral (lower half, formerly called Commodore)
Captain
Commander
Lieutenant Commander
Lieutenant
Lieutenant, junior grade
Ensign
Chief Warrant Officers (W-4, W-3, W-2)

ENLISTED PERSONNEL
Master Chief Petty Officer
Senior Chief Petty Officer
Chief Petty Officer
Petty Officer First Class
Petty Officer Second Class
Petty Officer Third Class
Seaman
Seaman Apprentice
Seaman Recruit

The Reserves

The Army, Navy, and Air Force reserves all work in fundamentally the same fashion as each other. Reservists train for different amounts of time each year, depending upon where they fall in the "mobilization scenario":

DRILLING RESERVES: These people are paid for their time and, theoretically, should be the first to be called up—although special needs (i.e., medical reasons) might dictate pulling reservists from other areas. These reservists are divided into two categories:

Category A: They train one weekend a month, and two weekends sometime during the year.

Category B: They train one day a month, and ten to fifteen days during the year.

DRILLING RESERVES: These are unpaid reservists who are accruing "retirement points." In other words, any time in which they serve gets applied to the benefits they'll receive when they retire. There is only one category here:

Category D: They train one day a month and two weekends during the year.

INACTIVE RESERVES: This type requires no drilling, offers no pay, and earns its members only a relatively small amount of retirement time. There is just one category for inactive reservists as well:

Category H: No training.

Representatives of each of these services claim they don't have any idea why there are no categories C, E, F, or G, although one official suggests that they're being held for possible variations in the training and pay setup.

Being held in reserve, you might say.

The Draft

During the Revolutionary War, local militias drafted young men to fight the British. However, it wasn't until the Civil War that a national conscription act was passed in both the North and South, with doctors, clergy, and state officials being the only ones exempted from service—although in the North, young men *could* pay someone three hundred dollars to take their place.

The draft has had a spotty history since then and, since 1973, has been inoperative. However, draft classifications are still on the books. Should conscription ever return, here are the current classifications:

CLASS	WHO IS INCLUDED
1-A	Available to serve.
1-A-M	Available for medical, dental, and other specialized categories.
1-A-O	Conscientious objector; noncombatant military service only.
1-C	Present member of the armed forces, Public Health Service, or National Oceanic and Atmospheric Administration.
1-H	Exempt from induction for reasons other than those specified in different categories.
1-O	Conscientious objector; nonmilitary service only.
1-W	Conscientious objector; no service at all.
2-A-M	Medical, dental, or other specialist; deferred due to community obligations.
2-D	Deferred; theological student.
2-M	Deferred; medical student.
3-A	Deferred; sole support of others.
4-A	Registrant who has already served in the military.
4-B	Deferred; public service official.
4-C	Alien.
4-D	Clergy.

CLASS	WHO IS INCLUDED
4-F	Registrant unqualified (usually due to a medical problem).
4-G	Inducted only in the event of war.
4-W	Conscientious objector who has already served in a nonmilitary capacity.

Regarding the gaps in the lettering, some letters are being reserved for possible future use, while several classifications—such as 2S, the student deferment so popular during the war in Vietnam—have been retired.

Soviet Armed Forces

There are three branches of the Soviet Armed Forces, and their ranks are as follows. Note: KGB ranks are identical to those of the Army, except that the top-ranked KGB officer is Colonel General.

ARMY:
Generalissimo of the Soviet Union
Marshal of the Soviet Union
Chief Marshal of Artillery
General (three kinds: Marshal of Artillery, of Communications, and of Engineers)
General-Colonel
General-Lieutenant
General-Major
Colonel
Lieutenant Colonel
Major
Captain
Senior Lieutenant
Lieutenant
Junior Lieutenant
Praporshchik
Starshina
Senior Sergeant
Sergeant
Junior Sergeant
Corporal
Private

AIR FORCE:
Chief Marshal of the Air Force
Marshal of the Air Force
General-Colonel
General-Lieutenant

General-Major
Colonel
Lieutenant Colonel
Major
Captain
Senior Lieutenant
Lieutenant
Junior Lieutenant
Michman
Principal Shipboard Starshina
Principal Starshina
Starshina First Step
Starshina Second Step
Senior Sailor
Sailor

NAVY:
Admiral of the Soviet Union
Admiral of the Fleet
Admiral
Vice Admiral
Rear Admiral
Captain First Rank
Captain Second Rank
Captain Third Rank
Captain Lieutenant
Senior Lieutenant
Lieutenant
Junior Lieutenant
Michman
Principal Shipboard Starshina
Principal Starshina
Starshina First Step
Starshina Second Step
Senior Sailor
Sailor

German Army Ranks in World War II

Finishing out the military rankings are two for the books . . . the history books.

During World War II, the German army ranks from lowest to highest were:

RANK	U. S. EQUIVALENT
MANNSCHAFTEN	**MEN**
1. Schütze	Private
2. Oberschütze	Senior private
3. Gefreiter	Lance Corporal
4. Obergefreiter	Corporal
UNTEROFFIZIER OHNE PORTEPEE	**JUNIOR NCOS**
1. Unteroffizier	Lance Sergeant
2. Unterfeldwebel	Sergeant
UNTEROFFIZIER MIT PORTEPEE	**SENIOR NCOS**
1. Feldwebel	Sergeant major
LEUTNANTE	**LIEUTENANTS**
1. Leutnant	Second Lieutenant
2. Oberleutnant	Lieutenant
HAPTLEUTE	**CAPTAINS**
1. Hauptmann	Captain
STABSOFFIZIERE	**FIELD OFFICERS**
1. Major	Major
2. Oberstleutnant	Lieutenant colonel
3. Oberst	Colonel
GENERALE	**GENERALS**
1. Generalmajor	Major general
2. Generalleutnant	Lieutenant general
3. General	General

4. Generaloberst   Colonel general
5. Generalfeldmarschall   General field-marshal

These are the broadest of headings, for there were often dozens of types of soldiers. For example, under sergeant major are the following types: Sanitätsoberfeldwebel (Battalion sergeant major, medical troops), Oberbeschlagmesiter (Battalion farrier sergeant major), Oberfeuerwerker (Battalion ordnance sergeant-major), Walloberfeldwebel (Fortifications battalion sergeant major), Festungspionieroberfeldwebel (Fortress engineer battalion sergeant major), and twelve others. There were also countless ranks for administration officials, one of the most mind-boggling of which is Direktor bei der Heeresfeuerwerker und Panzertruppenschle (Director of the Army Ordnance and Panzer [armored] Troop Schools).

Ranks During the Civil War

When the Southern states seceded from the Union and formed the Confederacy, they quickly built up their own army and naval forces for the struggle ahead.

The armies came from local militia already in place, and the ranks were the same as in the Union army. But the navy had to be built virtually from scratch and, to signify its individuality, the Confederacy took this opportunity to create some unique ranks:

UNION	CONFEDERACY
Ensign	Passed Midshipman
Master	Master
Lieutenant	Lieutenant
Lieutenant Commander	(no equivalent)
Commander	Commander
Captain	Captain
Commodore	Flag Officer
Rear Admiral	(no equivalent)

Nuclear Missiles

There are eight major systems for the delivery of nuclear weapons, each having its own range. From the most far-reaching, these are:

TYPE	RANGE (maximum, in miles)
1. Intercontinental Ballistic Missiles (ICBMs)	9,300
2. Long-Range Bombers	7,450
3. Medium-Range Bombers	6,800
4. Submarine Launched Ballistic Missiles (SLBMs)	5,650 (includes both range of the projectile and distance of vessel from home base)
5. Intermediate (a.k.a. Medium Range Ballistic Missiles (IRBMs)	3,100
6. Short-Range Aircraft	2,360
7. Short-Range Ballistic Missiles (SRBMs)	570
8. Artillery	13.2

Army Groupings

I f you saw the movie *Platoon*, but still don't know how many soldiers are *in* a platoon, help is on the way! In the Army, you'll find:

GROUPING	MINIMUM COMPOSITION
Unit	2 soldiers
Squad	10 soldiers
Platoon	4 squads
Company	2 platoons
Battalion	2 companies
Group	2 battalions
Brigade	2 groups
Division	3 brigades
Corps	2 divisions
Field Army	2 corps

Note: in the artillery, a company is referred to as a battery. However, in the cavalry, a company is known as a troop, and a battalion is a squadron.

In the Air Force, the groupings are:

UNIT	MINIMUM COMPOSITION
Flight	2 aircraft
Squadron	2 flights
Group	2 squadrons
Wing	2 groups
Air Division	2 wings
Air Force	2 air divisions
Air Command	air divisions and all support units and personnel

In the Navy, the units are:

UNIT	MINIMUM COMPOSITION
Division	4 ships
Squadron	2 divisions
Fleet	2 squadrons

Although a convoy has come to mean civilian ships accompanied by military ships, it can also be applied to two or more naval vessels.

MUSIC

The Musical Scale

Despite what Julie Andrews sang, the musical scale has nothing to do with female deers, a drop of golden sun, or anything else pastoral. The syllables were devised by eleventh-century monk Guido d'Arezzo, who based the names on a Latin hymn that exalted John the Baptist.

The only difference between the Latin and English versions are "ut" ("do") and "si" ("ti"). The changes were made when d'Arezzo translated the scale to Italian.

MUSICAL SYLLABLE	HYMN PHRASE
Ut	Ut queant laxis (As he spreads out)
Re	Resonare fibris (Resounding fiber [of the man himself])
Mi	Mira gestorum (Wonderful "carrying on")
Fa	Famuli tuorum (Servant [of God] who is observed [by people])
Sol	Solve polluti (Pure of soul)
La	Labi reatum (Sound defendant [before the Romans])
Si	Sancte Iohannes (Holy John)

Vocal Ranges

The human voice is as sophisticated and diverse as any musical instrument. From high to low, here are the vocal ranges and their subdivisions:

SOPRANO: From the Italian "sovrano," or "highest." The usual reach is two octaves up from the B-flat below middle C.
    Coloratura: Highest of all, with a bell-like pitch.
    Lyric (a.k.a. *Leggiero*): High and delicate.
    SFOGATO: High and reedy, thinner than ordinary lyric. From the Italian for "unburdened."
    SPINTO: The lowest range of the lyric voice, more dramatic than others.
    Dramatic: Not as high, but powerful.
    DUGAZON: Dramatic, but in a coquettish way; less powerful than sly. (Named for Louise Rosalie Dugazon, who specialized in these roles).
    FALCON: Dramatic, with great flare. (Named for Marie-Cornelie Falcon).

MEZZO-SOPRANO: Female voice between soprano and alto, though closer to the latter.

ALTO (a.k.a. CONTRALTO): From Latin for "high," the lowest type of female voice (roughly comparable to counter-tenor in the male). Range is usually two octaves up from the E below middle C.

TENOR: From the Italian "teneo," to "hold," because the tenor held the tune in most medieval music. The range is an octave below and above middle C.
    Counter-tenor: Extremely high, usually a falsetto.
    Trial: High and nasal. (Named for Antoine Trial).
    Tenor di grazia: High and graceful.
    Heldentenor (a.k.a. *Tenor di forza* and *tenor robusto*): High but heroic.

Spinto: High but able to drop to a more dramatic range.

Tenor buffo: Low tenor; invariably used in comic roles.

BARITONE: From the Greek for "heavy tone." A male voice that has a range of two octaves above the A nine notes below middle C.

Baritone-Martin: High baritone, nearly a tenor. (Named after Jean Blaise Martin).

Bass-baritone: Situated between baritone and bass.

BASS (a.k.a. **BASSO**): Lowest voice, able to reach two octaves up from the E twelve notes below middle C.

Basso cantante: A relatively high, lyric bass.

Basso buffo: A bass that can be cantante but has a lower bottom range.

Basso profundo (a.k.a. **Contra-basso):** The lowest voice there is.

Note: the range of the castrati—male singers castrated in their youth, thus "locking in" their high voices—encompassed high soprano to low contralto.

The Orchestra

If Julie Andrews's grasp of music was shaky, Robert Preston's was even worse. Despite his claims in *The Music Man*, a modern symphony orchestra is comprised of the following instruments:

INSTRUMENT	NUMBER
First violins	17
Second violins	16
Violas	12
Cellos	12
Double basses	9
French horns	6
Trumpets	4
Trombones	4
Percussion	4
Bassoons	3
Oboes	3
Flutes	3
Clarinets	3
Harps	2
Bass clarinet	1
English horn	1
Tuba	1
Piccolo	1
Contrabassoon	1
Piano or organ	1

Musical Notes

If you can read music, but can't remember why the notes look different—some solid, some open, some with stems, some not—here's a refresher course:

NOTE	TYPE	DESCRIPTION
Breve	Twice a semibreve	Open note between two vertical bars, no stem
Semibreve	A whole note	Open note, no stem
Minim	A half-note	Open note with a stem
Crotchet	A quarter-note	Solid note with a stem
Quaver	An eighth-note	Solid note with a stem and flag (or tail)
Semiquaver	A sixteenth-note	Solid note with a stem and two flags
Demisemiquaver	A thirty-second note	Solid note with a stem and three flags
Hemidemisemiquaver	A sixty-fourth note	Solid note with a stem and four flags

The Sounds of Music

N ow that you can recognize the notes, what's all that foreign scribble underneath for? It tells you just how loudly you should play that Chopin étude or Beethoven Sonata:

1. Fortississimo (fff): As loudly as possible
2. Fortissimo (ff): Very loudly
3. Forte (f): Loudly
4. Mezzo-forte (mf): Moderately loudly
5. Mezzo (m): Medium loudly
6. Mezzo-piano (mp): Medium softly
7. Piano (p): Softly
8. Pianissimo (pp): Very softly
9. Pianississimo (ppp): As softly as you can

   Transitions from one to the other can be handled *piu forte* (pf), or from soft to loud; and *fortepiano* (fp), from loud to soft.

Musical Interpretation

At last, having mastered the notes and tempo, here are the instructions you'll find for interpretation and pacing:

1. Grave: Very slow to the point of solemnity
2. Largo: Very slow and dignified
3. Adagio: Very slow, but not dolorous
4. Lento: Slow
5. Andante: At a slow walking pace
6. Andantino: At a steady walking pace
7. Moderato: At a brisk walking pace
8. Allegretto: With animation
9. Allegro: Lively
10. Vivace: Fast
11. Presto: Very fast
12. Prestissimo: Extremely fast

OCCULT

Witchcraft

Witchcraft evolved from ancient pagan rites that celebrated the earth and its interconnection with human beings. Animals and, occasionally, people were slain by pagans to guarantee the fertility of the earth. Likewise, these pagans believed that the issue of the soil—the flora, the fauna, and the minerals—could be used to influence human fate.

The coming of Christianity drove many of these pagan groups underground, where they have remained more or less hidden. Today, these witches—the word "witch" derives from the Old English *wicce*, "bad"—are organized into groups of thirteen known as *covens*. There are four grades of witches. From the lowest to highest:

WITCH: One who is permitted to study what is referred to today as "the natural religion" of earth-worship.

PRIESTESS OR PRIEST: One who has mastered the basics of the art, and is permitted to enter a coven.

WITCH QUEEN (female) **OR MAGUS** (male): A high-ranking member of the coven, permitted to initiate priestesses and priests.

HIGH PRIESTESS OR HIGH PRIEST: The leader of a coven, and the only one permitted to carry a broomstick . . . which, incidentally, represents the phallus, itself a symbol of fertility.

The Laws of Witches

The Greek god Hermes was associated with astrology and magic. The Romans adapted Hermes for their own, as they did much of Greek culture, and worked many rites and spells in his name. These rituals eventually made their way to the druids of Europe and, from there, came to the witches of America.

Throughout the centuries, witches have regarded the Seven Hermetic Laws as the foundation for their art. They are as sacrosanct to witches as the Ten Commandments are to Judeo-Christian peoples, and are paraphrased below from the most important.

1. **THE LAW OF MENTALISM:** We are all linked to the Divine Consciousness that pervades the universe, and each of us has the ability to tap its knowledge.

2. **THE LAW OF CORRESPONDENCE:** There are realms beyond the visible, sensory world, and we must try to be in synch with them. We as witches must often go looking beyond our tangible sphere for energy.

3. **THE LAW OF VIBRATION:** Nothing is at rest, and every object vibrates (albeit, imperceptibly) at its own speed. (Witches believe that the energies and auras given off by people and things is directly related to this movement.)

4. **THE LAW OF POLARITY:** Everything has an opposite—good, evil; lie, truth; love, hate—and one can be transformed to the other by using the waves that pass between them.

5. **THE LAW OF RHYTHM:** Everything is cyclical, and can be understood and influenced if one gets in tune with its "beat."

6. **THE LAW OF GENDER:** All living things have male and female sides that generate different forms of energy. Recognizing these is a key to understanding others and their strengths and weaknesses.

7. **THE LAW OF CAUSE AND EFFECT:** Nothing happens of its own volition; there is a cause for everything. So before affecting one part of the universal "web," a witch must consider what *else* might affect it, and how it will affect other things.

Wizardry

Though magicians, like witches, allegedly have been with us since the dawn of civilization, it wasn't until 1890 that Britain's magician's guild, the Hermetic Order of the Golden Dawn, established actual rankings for wizards. They created three Orders of practitioners and broke them down in the following "grades," listed from the least to the most powerful:

OUTER ORDER
1. Neophyte
2. Zelator
3. Theoricus
4. Practicus
5. Philosophus

SECOND ORDER
6. Adeptus Minor
7. Adeptus Major
8. Adeptus Exemptus

THIRD ORDER
9. Magister
10. Magus
11. Ipsissimus

The Tree of Life

The Cabala is a collection of obscure, symbolic, and often opaque Jewish mystic knowledge and tradition passed orally from one generation to the next. Today, many of its teachings are highly regarded by mystics and occultists the world over. Indeed, Freud is said to have delved deeply into its teachings when developing his psychoanalytical theories.

One of the key beliefs for Cabalists is the truth to be found in the Tree of Life. It is, in short, a map: by mastering the qualities found in each of these ten spheres (a.k.a. *sefiroth*) in turn, one can achieve the godhead. From the roots:

MALKHUTH: The physical body; health.

YESOD: The personality.

HOD: The powers of logic and reason.

NETSAH: Our animal needs, passions, and senses.

TIFERETH: Also known as *Rahamin,* the life force or energy that drives the above-mentioned spheres.

GEBURAH: Also known as *Pachad* or *Din,* the destructive nature in all of us.

HESED: Also known as *Gedulah,* the quality of love and mercy.

BINAH: The soul; the divine spark that impels us to achieve greatness.

HOKHMAH: Creative thought, which is considered to be the father of all the great works we achieve.

KETHER: The crown; the ultimate unity of all aspects of human nature.

Exorcism

During the Dark Ages, when people sneezed, they believed they were expelling a spirit that had briefly possessed them. When epileptics had fits, many who watched their pained contortions were convinced that the epileptics were possessed by demons.

We now know better, of course, but many people still believe that humans can be possessed by the devil. Since 1614, when the Roman Catholic Church first composed its *Rituale Romanum,* the ritual for driving out a demon from its victim has been clearly described. Upon being ushered into the presence of one possessed, the exorcist performs his tasks in this sequence:

CONVERSATION: The exorcist engages the demon in quiet conversation and, in the name of God, orders it to leave.

HOLY SYMBOLS: If reason fails to drive away the demon (and it rarely does), symbols such as a cross or Bible are held before the victim.

COMMANDS: Should symbols fail, the exorcist now speaks "harshly" with the demon, commanding it to depart.

THE BIBLE: Passages from the Bible are read. The exorcist is no longer free to converse with the demon, but must read forcefully. The reading continues until the devil is gone.

The exorcist is advised to keep his distance, lest the spirit leave its victim and claim him.

In most cases, the strength of the exorcist's own convictions is what determines the effectiveness of the rite.

Seances

A medium is a person who is said to be able to communicate with the dead. More accurately, the dead communicate *through* the medium, using his or her vocal chords to address the living. Sometimes the medium's voice is heard; frequently, though, it is supposedly the voice of the deceased.

When a medium invites people in for a seance, the experience can be as traumatic for the medium as for the listeners. The spiritual host goes through several stages of getting his or her own self out of the way in order to let the soul of the dead come through unhindered. While the first four stages can often be accomplished in under a minute, it usually takes closer to four or five minutes.

STAGES

1. **CLEARING:** The mind is emptied of all things.
2. **SLOWING:** The body relaxes, with the heart rate dropping.
3. **WITHDRAWING:** The soul of the medium begins to retreat into some unknown corner of the body.
4. **PHASING:** The spirit communicates through the body.
5. **DEPHASING:** The spirit departs, often in a hurry.
6. **RESTORING:** The medium once again takes control of his or her body.

Superstitions

When the English colonists came to America, they brought with them superstitions that had been a part of their culture for hundreds of years. Though the origins of these hierarchal beliefs have been lost, many of them are with us still.

Perhaps the most famous of these is the skirt-button form of fortune-telling. When a young girl puts on a skirt for the first time, her mother tells her to count the buttons; the number will determine the kind of man she will marry. From one button to eight, they are:

A doctor, a lawyer, a merchant, a chief,
A rich man, a poor man, a beggar-man, thief.

(Obviously, the wise mother would have made certain that there were no more than five buttons on her daughter's skirt!)

In colonial times, a better-known superstition involved crows. Upon moving into a new home and looking out the window for the first time, here's what people expected for the day depending upon the number of crows they saw:

One means anger, two bring mirth.
Three a wedding, four a birth.
Five is heaven, six is hell.
But seven's the very Devil's own sell [soul].

Not surprisingly, the moon has its own laws of order, which date back to the days of the Celts. These superstitions have been passed to us via *The Cotton Manuscript*, which is kept in the British Museum. Tradition holds that the first ten days after the new moon affect us accordingly:

NEW MOON: A good day to start a new undertaking. To be born on this day means you'll have a long and successful life.

SECOND DAY: The best day for farmers to begin plowing the fields, or for anyone to buy or sell something.

THIRD DAY: Children born on this day will die young; criminals committing a crime on this day will definitely be captured.

FOURTH DAY: Builders and politicians should begin new projects on this day.

FIFTH DAY: An ideal day on which to conceive a child. The weather for the rest of the month will be most like the weather on this day.

SIXTH DAY: A fine day for fishing or hunting.

SEVENTH DAY: Lovers who meet on this day will lead happy lives together.

EIGHTH DAY: If you get sick today, you'll almost certainly die from it.

NINTH DAY: Look at the moon tonight, and you're likely to go mad.

TENTH DAY: Children born on this day will grow up to be nomadic, unable to find happiness in any spot, on any job, or with any spouse.

RELIGION

Gods and Goddesses

The ancient Greeks don't quite agree on how the gods and our world came into being. According to the poet Orpheus, Time always existed, and it spawned Chaos, which consisted of Night, Mist, and Air. Mist begat an egg, which split and became Heaven and Earth, with Eros crawling out from within. On the other hand, Hesiod believed that Chaos came first, spawning Erebus (Darkness), Nyx (night), and Gaea (Earth). Gaea then gave birth to Uranus who, by her, became the father of the gods. Yet Homer subscribed to the notion that Oceanus always existed, and that he alone eventually gave birth to everything.

Here is the order of Olympian births that followed the arrival of Gaea. (At least on this, everyone seems to agree.) The importance of the god, goddess, or demigod is directly related to both the order of his or her birth and to his or her parentage. For example, it's better to be the offspring of Zeus and a goddess rather than the child of some lesser gods, although the issue of two gods outweighs that of Zeus and a mortal woman.

(Note: when Rome swallowed up the Greeks in the second century B.C., they also adapted the Greeks' religion. The Roman names for the "borrowed" Greek gods are noted parenthetically.)

Though Hera was the sister and wife of Zeus, Zeus had many lovers, as is shown. Most of his partners were titanesses, meaning other children of Uranus and Gaea.

PARENTS	OFFSPRING	RESPONSIBILITIES
Gaea (Terra)	Uranus (Coelus)	
Uranus and Gaea	Chronus (Saturn)	
	Rhea (Cybele)	
Chronus and Rhea	Zeus (Jupiter)	King of the gods
	Hera (Juno)	Queen of the gods
	Poseidon (Neptune)	God of the sea
	Hades (Pluto)	God of the underworld
	Demeter (Ceres)	Goddess of agriculture
	Hestia (Vesta)	Goddess of the hearth
Zeus and Hera	Ares (Mars)	God of war
	Hephaestus (Vulcan)	God of fire
Zeus and Leto	Apollo (Apollo)	God of the sun
	Artemis (Diana)	Goddess of the moon and hunting
Zeus and Metis	Athene, or Pallas Athene (Minerva)	Goddess of wisdom
Zeus and Dione	Aphrodite (Venus)	Goddess of love
Zeus and Maia	Hermes (Mercury)	Messenger of the gods
Zeus and Semele	Dionysus (Bacchus)	God of wine
Aphrodite and Ares	Eros (Cupid)	God of love
Zeus and Alcmene	Heracles (Hercules)	Demigod; hero
Zeus and Danae	Perseus	Demigod; hero
Aphrodite and Anchises (a mortal)	Aeneas	Demigod; hero

The Act of Creation

Unlike the ancient Greeks, the Judeo-Christian religions have no problem with the story and order of creation: the Bible spells it all out clearly. According to the Old Testament, all things were created in the following sequence:

DAY ONE
"The heaven and the earth."
"Light . . . and God called the light Day, and the darkness He called Night."

DAY TWO
"A firmament in the midst of the waters [to] divide the waters from the waters."

DAY THREE
"Grass, the herb-yielding seed, and the fruit tree."

DAY FOUR
"Two great lights; the greater light to rule the day, and the lesser light to rule the night; He made the stars also."

DAY FIVE
"Every living creature that moveth, which the waters brought forth abundantly . . . and every winged fowl."

DAY SIX
"Cattle . . . and every thing that creepeth upon the earth."
"Man . . . male and female."

Angels

The rankings of angels was formalized by religious scholars in the fourth century, who based the hierarchy on the writings of Paul, among others (i.e., Eph. 1:21, Col. 1:16, etc.). They consist of nine orders, and are grouped in three hierarchies, a.k.a. choirs. From the most powerful and hallowed, these are:

FIRST HIERARCHY:
Seraphim
Cherubim
Thrones

SECOND HIERARCHY:
Dominions
Principalities
Powers

THIRD HIERARCHY:
Virtues
Archangels
Angels

Devils

Just as there are hierarchies of angels, so there are levels for their fallen kinfolk, devils. One of history's most noted exorcists, Father Sebastien Michaelis, described the rankings in his *Admirable History* (1612). He also revealed the sins of which each devil was in charge.

THE DEVIL:
Lucifer
FIRST HIERARCHY:
Beelzebub (pride)
Leviathan (sins "directly repugnant unto faith")
Asmodeus (luxuriousness and wantonness)
Balberith (homicides, quarrels, blasphemy)
Astaroth (idleness and sloth)
Verrine (impatience)
Gressil (impurity and uncleanness)
Sonneillon (hatred)
SECOND HIERARCHY:
Carreau (hard-heartedness)
Carnivean (obscenity)
Oeillet (temptation to "break the vow of poverty")
Rosier (causes people to fall hopelessly in love—implicitly, abandoning god for the flesh)
Verrier (disobedience)
THIRD HIERARCHY:
Belias (arrogance)
Olivier (mercilessness toward the poor)
Iuvart (this devil is inactive, trapped in the body of a nun at Louviers)

According to *Compendium Maleficarum* (1608) by Friar Francesco-Maria Guazzo, six different kinds of demons serve the above-mentioned princes. From the most powerful, they are:

1. **FIRE DEVILS,** who live in the upper air and help supervise the other five groups of demons.
2. **AERIAL DEVILS,** who inhabit the air around us, and thus have the most direct access to us.
3. **TERRESTRIAL DEVILS,** who dwell in the woods, fields, and forests.
4. **AQUEOUS DEVILS,** who reside in rivers, lakes, and seas.
5. **SUBTERRANEAN DEVILS,** who live in caves and mountains.
6. **HELIOPHOBIC DEVILS,** light-haters who appear only at night.

The Hierarchy of the Catholic Church

Jesus's apostle Peter went to Rome circa A.D. 42, where he founded the Roman Catholic Church. Martyred in A.D. 67, he was subsequently elevated to sainthood.

Since Peter, there have been 262 popes (or heads of the Roman Catholic Church), all of them selected by the College of Cardinals. These and the other ranks in the church, in descending order of importance, are as follows:

POPE: He has many titles: Bishop of Rome, Vicar of Jesus Christ, Successor of St. Peter, Prince of the Apostles, Supreme Pontiff of the Universal Church, Patriarch of the West, Primate of Italy, Archbishop and Metropolitan of the Roman Province, and Sovereign of the State of Vatican City.

CARDINAL: A member of the College of Cardinals, appointed by the Pope. In turn, the cardinals are responsible for selecting a new Pope upon the death of the old. There are three kinds of cardinals, from highest to lowest:
Cardinal Bishop
Cardinal Priest
Cardinal Deacon

ARCHBISHOP: A bishop who is responsible for an archdiocese or archbishopric, consisting of more than one diocese or see, or one such district of unusual size.

BISHOP: Religious leader of a diocese.

MONSIGNOR: A priest who has been honored with a special title for his extraordinary service.

PRIEST: Head of a parish, a district that has its own church.

DEACON: A cleric with duties in a parish, but ranked below a priest.

Other church leaders, who serve in individual orders, are:

RECTOR: A cleric in charge of a college or congregation.

ABBOT: The head of a monastery.

PRIOR: An officer of a monastic order who ranks below an abbot.

Members of religious orders—people such as monks and nuns—hold no rank, per se, but are the equivalent of privates in the army of God.

Jewish, Islamic, and Hindu Calendars

The names of the months in these three major religions are as follows. They're listed so that they correspond to our year of January to December, although the first month of the religion's year is marked with an asterisk (*).

JEWISH:

1. Shebat	7. Ab
2. Adar	8. Elul
3. Nisan	*9. Tishri
4. Iyar	10. Heshvan
5. Sivan	11. Kislev
6. Tammuz	12. Tebet

ISLAMIC:

*1. Muharram	7. Rajab
2. Safar	8. Sha'ban
3. Rabi I	9. Ramadan
4. Rabi II	10. Shawwal
5. Jumada I	11. Dhu'l-Qa'da
6. Jumada II	12. Dhu'l-hijja

HINDU:

1. Magha	7. Sravana
2. Phalguna	8. Bhadrapada
*3. Caitra	9. Asvina
4. Vaisakha	10. Karttika
5. Jyaistha	11. Margasivsa
6. Asadha	12. Pansa

SCIENCE

The Periodic Table

W̶hat book of lists and laws would be complete without the building blocks of all matter?

From the lightest elements upward:

ELEMENT	MEANING (Greek = G, Latin = L)	NUMBER	SYMBOL	WEIGHT
Hydrogen	G: "water producer"	1	H	1.00794
Helium	G: "sun"	2	He	4.002602
Lithium	G: "stone"	3	Li	6.941
Beryllium	G: "beryl"	4	Be	9.012182
Boron	Persian: "borax"	5	B	10.811
Carbon	L: "charcoal"	6	C	12.011
Nitrogen	G: "saltpeter producer"	7	N	14.00674
Oxygen	G: "acid producer"	8	O	15.9994
Fluorine	L: "flow"	9	F	18.998403
Neon	G: "new"	10	Ne	20.1797
Sodium	English: "soda"	11	Na	22.989768
Magnesium	Magnesia, in Thessaly	12	Mg	24.3050
Aluminum	L: "alum"	13	Al	26.981539
Silicon	L: "flint"	14	Si	28.0855
Phosphorus	G: "light bringing"	15	P	30.973762

ELEMENT	MEANING (Greek = G, Latin = L)	NUMBER	SYMBOL	WEIGHT
Sulfur	L: "sulfurum"	16	S	32.066
Chlorine	G: "green"	17	Cl	35.4527
Argon	G: "inactive"	18	Ar	39.948
Potassium (a.k.a. Kalium)	English: "potash"	19	K	39.0983
Calcium	L: "lime"	20	Ca	40.078
Scandium	Scandinavia	21	Sc	44.955910
Titanium	L: "sons of the earth"	22	Ti	47.88
Vanadium	Norse: Vanadis (goddess of beauty)	23	V	50.9415
Chromium	G: "color"	24	Cr	51.9961
Manganese	L: "magnet"	25	Mn	54.93805
Iron (a.k.a. Ferrum)	Anglo-Saxon "iren"	26	Fe	55.847
Cobalt	German: "goblin"	27	Co	58.93320
Nickel	German: "devil's copper"	28	Ni	58.69
Copper	Cyprus	29	Cu	63.546
Zinc	German: "zink"	30	Zn	65.39
Gallium	L: France	31	Ga	69.723
Germanium	L: Germany	32	Ge	72.61
Arsenic	G: "virile"	33	As	74.92159
Selenium	G: "moon"	34	Se	78.96
Bromine	G: "stench"	35	Br	79.904
Krypton	G: "hidden"	36	Kr	83.80
Rubidium	L: "red"	37	Rb	85.4678
Strontium	Strontian, in Scotland	38	Sr	87.62
Yttrium	Ytterby, in Sweden	39	Y	88.90585
Zirconium	Persian: "gold-colored"	40	Zr	91.224

ELEMENT	MEANING (Greek = G, Latin = L)	NUMBER	SYMBOL	WEIGHT
Niobium	Niobe, daughter of Tantalus, king of Phrygia	41	Nb	92.90638
Molybdenum	G: lead	42	Mo	95.94
Technetium	G: "artificial"	43	Tc	97.9072
Ruthenium	Ruthenia, in USSR	44	Ru	101.7
Rhodium	G: "rose"	45	Rh	102.90550
Palladium	Pallas, the asteroid	46	Pd	106.42
Silver (a.k.a. Argentum)	Anglo-Saxon "seolfor"	47	Ag	107.868
Cadmium	G: "calamine"	48	Cd	112.411
Indium	English: "indigo"	49	In	114.82
Tin (a.k.a. Stannum)	Anglo-Saxon "tin"	50	Sn	118.710
Antimony (a.k.a. Stibium)	L: "antimonium" (coined to describe the element)	51	Sb	121.75
Tellurium	L: "earth"	52	Te	127.60
Iodine	G: "violet"	53	I	126.90447
Xenon	G: "stranger"	54	Xe	131.29
Caesium	L: "blue-gray"	55	Cs	132.90543
Barium	G: "heavy"	56	Ba	137.327
Lanthanum	G: "conceal"	57	La	138.9055
Cerium	Ceres, the asteroid	58	Ce	140.115
Praseodymium	G: "green twin"	59	Pr	140.90765
Neodymium	G: "new twin"	60	Nd	144.24
Promethium	G: Prometheus	61	Pm	144.9127

ELEMENT	MEANING (Greek = G, Latin = L)	NUMBER	SYMBOL	WEIGHT
Samarium	Colonel M. Samarski, Russian engineer	62	Sm	150.36
Europium	Europe	63	Eu	151.965
Gadolinium	Johan Gadolin	64	Gd	157.25
Terbium	Ytterby, Sweden ("ter")	65	Tb	158.92534
Dysprosium	G: "hard to get at"	66	Dy	162.50
Holmium	L: "Holmia" (Stockholm)	67	Ho	164.93032
Erbium	Ytterby, Sweden ("erb")	68	Er	167.26
Thulium	L: "Northland" (Thule)	69	Tm	168.93421
Ytterbium	Ytterby, Sweden	70	Yb	173.04
Lutetium	L: "Lutetia" (Paris)	71	Lu	174.967
Hafnium	"Hafnia" (Copenhagen)	72	Hf	178.49
Tantalum	Tantalus, a Greek king	73	Ta	180.9479
Tungsten (a.k.a. Wolfram)	Swedish: "heavy stone"	74	W	183.85
Rhenium	L: "Rhenus" (Rhine)	75	Re	186.207
Osmium	G: "odor"	76	Os	190.2
Iridium	L: "rainbow"	77	Ir	192.22
Platinum	Spanish: "small silver"	78	Pt	195.08
Gold (a.k.a. Aurum)	Anglo-Saxon "gold"	79	Au	196.96654
Mercury (a.k.a. Hydrargyrum)	Mercury, Roman god	80	Hg	200.59

ELEMENT	MEANING (Greek = G, Latin = L)	NUMBER	SYMBOL	WEIGHT
Thallium	G: "a budding twig"	81	Tl	205.3833
Lead (a.k.a. Plumbum)	Anglo-Saxon "lead"	82	Pb	207.2
Bismuth	German: "white matter"	83	Bi	208.98037
Polonium	Poland	84	Po	208.9824
Astatine	G: "unstable"	85	At	209.9871
Radon	L: "ray"	86	Rn	222.0176
Francium	France	87	Fr	223.0197
Radium	L: "ray"	88	Ra	226.0254
Actinium	G: "ray"	89	Ac	227.0278
Thorium	Thor, Norse god	90	Th	232.0381
Protactinium	G: "first"	91	Pa	231.0359
Uranium	Uranus, the planet	92	U	238.0289
Neptunium	Neptune, the planet	93	Np	237.0482
Plutonium	Pluto, the planet	94	Pu	244.0642
Americium	America	95	Am	243.0614
Curium	Pierre and Marie Curie	96	Cm	247.0703
Berkelium	Berkeley (California), U.S.	97	Bk	247.0703
Californium	California	98	Cf	251.0796
Einsteinium	Dr. Albert Einstein	99	Es	252.0829
Fermium	Dr. Enrico Fermi	100	Fm	257.0951
Mendelevium	Dmitri I. Mendeleyev	101	Md	258.0986
Nobelium	Alfred B. Nobel	102	No	259.1009
Lawrencium	Dr. Ernest O. Lawrence	103	Lr	260.11

ELEMENT	MEANING (Greek = G, Latin = L)	NUMBER	SYMBOL	WEIGHT
Unnilquadium	"104" (un-nil-quad)	104	Unq	261.1087
Unnilpentium	"105"	105	Unp	262.1138
Unnilhexium	"106"	106	Unh	262.1182
Unnilseptium	"107"	107	Uns	262.1229
Unniloctium	"108"	108	Uno	265.1302
Unnilennium	"109"	109	Une	266.1376

Though the names for elements 104–109 are as practical as they come, the International Union of Pure and Applied Chemistry are weighing the names Rutherfordium (Rf) and Kurchatovium (Ku) for 104, and Hahnium (Ha) and Nielsbohrium (Ns) for 105.

Only those elements listed up through Uranium occur naturally in nature.

Atomic Particles

When you discuss the size of an atom, you're talking *small*—an object with a radius of 10^{-10} millimeters in diameter, to be exact. Yet there's matter that's even smaller: the electron, which orbits the nucleus of the atom, is 10^{-15} millimeter in diameter!

Incredibly, there's matter that's smaller still, subatomic particles so minuscule they aren't even measured in terms of diameter but in terms of mass—in this case, MeV's, or million-electron-volts. (MeV's are actually a measure of energy, but when it's that tiny, the numbers for mass and energy become the same.)

There are more than one hundred such particles, most of which are so ephemeral they perish in *quintillionths* of a second; try measuring *that* on your stopwatch. These include Tau particles, Muons, Mesons, and other denizens of the subatomic realm.

Those subatomic particles that are stable (indeed, eternal, as far as we know) are listed below, from the largest to the smallest.

SUBATOMIC PARTICLE	MASS IN MEV'S
Proton	938.3
Antiproton	938.3
Quark (Strange)	102.2
Quark (Down)	3
Quark (Up)	1
Positron	.511
Electron	.511
Antineutrino	0
Neutrino	0
Graviton	0
Photon	0
Gluon	0

Electromagnetic Rays

Why will gamma rays fry you, while those from your Sony radio won't? It has to do with the length of the electromagnetic radiation; the distance between the "crests" of each wave, so to speak. The shorter the distance, the more power the waves pack, so the more cooked you'll get.

From the shortest (and deadliest):

Gamma Rays
X rays
Ultraviolet rays
Visible light
Infrared rays
Radio frequencies:
   EHF (extremely high frequency)
   SHF (super high frequency)
   UHF (ultra high frequency)
   VHF (very high frequency)
   HF (high frequency)
   MF (medium frequency)
   LF (low frequency)
   VLF (very low frequency)

The Color Spectrum

Color is determined by the wavelength of the light; that is, the distance between one crest of the light wave and the next (from 15 millionths of an inch for violet, to 28 millionths for red). We see a particular color when the object it's striking absorbs all but that particular wavelength.

Those colors that blend to form "white light" are listed below, grouped from the longest wavelength to the shortest. New colors such as brown or pink are created by making a surface (or paint or dye) that absorbs all wavelengths but the two or more that are mixed together.

1. Red
2. Orange
3. Yellow
4. Green
5. Blue
6. Indigo
7. Violet

Ever since Isaac Newton discovered the spectrum, Indigo frequently has been left off spectral listings. But if you do so, you can't create the wonderful mnemonic ROY G. BIV.

Atomic Fallout

When an atomic bomb goes off in the air, radioactive atoms link up with all the airborne dust and are carried in every direction. Eventually, all of it drops to Earth—hence the term *fallout*.

Fallout descends at different rates, depending upon what kind it is. The three types to look out for are:

1. **LOCAL FALLOUT:** This is comprised of the heaviest particles of dust and, thus, drops to Earth within minutes or hours of the blast. Local fallout comprises the bulk of nuclear dust.

2. **LONG-TERM FALLOUT:** Medium-weight fallout that is lofted into the lower regions of the atmosphere. It hangs there for several weeks before floating down to Earth. It can be carried hundreds of miles from where the bomb hits, or ground zero.

3. **GLOBAL FALLOUT:** Radiation that latches on to light dust particles and is propelled into the upper reaches of the atmosphere. This type of fallout can remain there for months or even years, and eventually might reach even the most distant regions of the planet.

Crude Oil

Thanks to all the headline-making, we know where crude petroleum comes from. However, what's much less known is how petroleum is refined. After all, it doesn't just go from the ground to your car or home.

When petroleum is run through a furnace and heated to eight hundred degrees Fahrenheit, the hydrocarbons that comprise the crude oil become vapor. These vapors rise into a fractioning tower—a structure that is super-hot at the bottom and gets progressively cooler toward the top. Since the hydrocarbons turn *back* into their liquid state at different temperatures, they condense at different levels of the tower, where they're collected on vast trays. From these trays, the now-solid hydrocarbons are funneled into pipes for further refining.

From bottom to top, this is the order in which the vapors become liquid once again:

1. Lubricating oil
2. Heating oil
3. Kerosene
4. Gasoline

The pH Scale

That mainstay of hair product commercials—"pH"—stands for "potential of hydrogen," and it's used to describe how acid or alkaline something is.

Devised by Soren Sorensen in 1909, the scale lists pH values from the most acid to the most alkaline, with "1" under acidity/alkalinity being neutral. In the chart below, the numbers to the right represent the numbers of moles (molecular weight, in grams) of hydrogen ions per cubic decimeter (i.e., per liter). Scientists actually have succeeded in producing substances with pH values of -1, -2, and -3, though these are of no practical value other than getting their creators published in academic journals.

PH VALUE	ACIDITY TO ALKALINITY	TYPICAL SUBSTANCE
0	10,000,000	Hydrochloric acid
1	1,000,000	Stomach acid
2	100,000	Soda pop
3	10,000	Grapefruit
4	1,000	Shampoo
5	100	Black coffee; acid rain; beer
6	10	Rain
7	1	Tap water
8	10	Blood
9	100	Eggs
10	1,000	Soap
11	10,000	Ammonia
12	100,000	Cleaning fluids
13	1,000,000	Caustic soda
14	10,000,000	Antacids

The Mineral Scale

Friedrich Mohs (1773–1839) was a German mineralogist who devised a scale that grades each mineral according to its softness. In other words, each mineral can be scratched by the next one in the list—a practical test indeed!

Here, then, is the Mohs scale, listing minerals from the softest to the hardest.

1. Talc
2. Gypsum
3. Calcite
4. Fluorite
5. Apatite
6. Orthoclase (feldspar)
7. Quartz
8. Topaz
9. Corundum
10. Diamond

SPORTS

Horse Gaits

Riding a horse professionally is a far cry from taking a turn on a pony at the local county fair. There are different gaits that, in competition, must be strictly adhered to. From the slowest to the quickest, these are:

1. **WALK:** A four-beat gait, meaning that each of the horse's hooves touches the ground separately. A walking horse averages five miles an hour.
2. **FOX TROT:** A slackening pace, which occurs when going from a trot to a walk.
3. **TROT:** A two-beat diagonal gait, meaning that the hind and foreleg diagonal to each other move together. There is a brief moment in the sequence when all four legs are off the ground. The trot averages nine miles an hour.
4. **PACE:** A two-beat gait in which the horse has a kind of waddling gait. In other words, the left foreleg and hindleg touch down together, and then the right legs do the same. The speed varies, depending upon the kind and condition of the horse.
5. **RACK:** A four-beat gait in which the horse is put through high, parade-like steps. This gait also varies in its speed.
6. **CANTER:** A three-beat gait, known to Western-style riders as the "lope." The canter averages twelve miles an hour.
7. **GALLOP:** A four-beat gait that is often described as an "unrestrained canter." This is a racing gait—rather than a gait used in horse shows—and averages twenty miles an hour.

Horse Racing

Putting the horseshoe on the other foot, when you're a casual watcher of a race like the Kentucky Derby, you've got to wonder what the animal did to get there. Most likely, it worked its way up through the ranks by running in successively more prestigious (and profitable) races. Classified as follows from the least prestigious:

CLAIMING RACES: These are so called because the horses racing here can be bought by another owner or, less frequently, by someone who's just come to enjoy the race. Owners race young horses here; so do owners whose horses are on the way down and are looking, at the very worst, to pick up a small purse. The average purchase price of a horse at these races is $5,000 as of this writing.

MAIDEN RACES: Slightly more prestigious than claiming races, these races are for talented horses who have not yet won a race. A horse can't race in this category again once it's won a Maiden race.

ALLOWANCE RACES: The horses in competition here have already won races. Many of them lack the speed to compete in big money races, and so remain at this level.

HANDICAP RACES: All of the entrants in these races are potential champions. To make sure each horse has an equal chance of winning, track handicappers assign them specific weights to carry; the weights are determined by their winning records. If the owner feels that the assigned weight will be too hard on the horse, he or she has the option to *scratch,* or withdraw, the animal from a given race.

STAKES RACES: These are the biggies, and only horses who have already won many races may enter. Owners must pay for their horses to race, but the purses that are awarded are large. Moreover, champions can go on to earn hefty stud fees for their owners. There are also stakes races for geldings, who compete far longer than those who have been retired to stud.

Bullfighting

One thing's for sure: Horses have it better than their four-legged brethren, the bulls.

Though bullfighting has been around in many countries for more than two thousand years, it's most closely identified with Spain: the so-called "fighting bull," the *toro de lidia* or *toro bravo*, originated there, and was later herded and bred by the Romans to pit against captives in the Colosseum.

After the fall of Rome, the Spanish turned bullfighting into a controversial national pastime. While peasants waved capes to catch the bull's eye, nobles rode around on horseback and poked it with lances. (One has to wonder how seriously the oppressed peasants tried to keep the animal away from their taskmasters.)

Today, a bullfight has a ritualistic cast of characters who enter the ring in this order:

PARTICIPANT	JOB
Banderillero	One to three banderilleros come out and swirl their capes before the bull—from a safe distance—to show the matador how the animal moves.
Matador	The human star of the show strolls out and, with his cape, encourages the bull to charge him. The closer the horns come to the matador, the happier the audience is.
Picador	After the matador has weathered several passes, two picadores ride out on horseback and stick the bull's neck with their lances, in order to weaken the animal's muscles. It's up to the matador, then, to use a sword to deliver the death blow.

Contrary to what many people believe—partly because it was perpetuated by Bizet's popular 1875 opera *Carmen*—the terms "matador" and "toreador" are not interchangeable. A toreador—technically, a *torero*—is any one of the men involved in the bullfight.

An even bigger misconception regards the color of the cape. Red has no impact whatsoever on the animal, since bulls are color blind. Rather, they charge because the waving mass indicates to them an opponent getting ready to charge.

Target Archery

Arrows are classified according to the lengths of their shafts, which range from twenty-two to thirty-two inches. The correct arrow length for an archer is determined by holding the arrow and one arm perpendicular to his body. The point of the arrow should extend just beyond his fingertips.

No rankings there, but there *is* an order to the arrangement of rings on a target. From outside in, the rankings in target archery are:

COLOR	POINTS
White outer ring	1
Next white ring	2
Black ring	3
Next black ring	4
Blue ring	5
Next blue ring	6
Red ring	7
Next red ring	8
Gold ring	9
Bull's-eye (gold)	10

In field archery, the targets are designed as follows:

COLOR	POINTS
Black outer ring	3
White middle ring	4
Black center ring	5

Distances in competition for men are 30, 50, 70, and 90 meters. For women, they are 30, 50, 60, and 70.

The target is 122 centimeters in diameter, save for when it's in the 30- and 50-meter rounds, at which time it's 80 centimeters.

Thanks to the National Archery Association for their help.

Golf

The ancient Greeks and Egyptians probably played some form of golf all those thousands of years ago (think of the great sand traps that could be had from the desert!). However, the sport can definitely be traced to the fourteenth-century European game of bandy ball, in which two adversaries hit a ball with golf-like clubs.

Today, golf is very much its own game, with equipment made to precise specifications. Players hit the ball with woods or irons. There are five woods that are commonly used in the game, with the number one wood—the largest—also being known as the driver. The irons are narrower than the woods, and are used for shorter shots. There are ten irons; the lower the number, the farther and lower the ball will go. Those with heads angled away from the vertical are:

IRON	ANGLE
Number Two	18 degrees
Number Three	21 degrees
Number Four	24 degrees
Number Five	27 degrees
Number Six	31 degrees
Number Seven	35 degrees
Pitching Wedge	48 degrees
Sand Wedge	55 degrees

Boxing Classes

If you yearn to capture a boxing title, but aren't keen on fighting Mike Tyson or Buster Douglas to get it, here are other classes you can enter, from heaviest to lightest.

CLASS	WEIGHT (in pounds)
1. Heavyweight	195 and up
2. Cruiserweight	up to 195
3. Light Heavyweight	up to 175
4. Middleweight	up to 160
5. Junior (a.k.a. Light) Middleweight	up to 154
6. Welterweight	up to 147
7. Junior (a.k.a. Light) Welterweight	up to 140
8. Lightweight	up to 135
9. Junior Lightweight	up to 130
10. Featherweight	up to 126
11. Junior Featherweight	up to 122
12. Bantamweight	up to 118
13. Flyweight	up to 112
14. Junior (a.k.a. Light) Flyweight	up to 108

Weightlifting and Wrestling Categories

Like boxers, weightlifters are categorized according to weight. The Amateur Athletic Union recognizes these levels:

CATEGORY	WEIGHT (in pounds)
Heavyweight	Over 198¼
Middle-Heavyweight	181½–198¼
Light-Heavyweight	165–181¼
Middleweight	148½–165¼
Lightweight	132–148½
Featherweight	123¼–132
Bantamweight	Under 123¼

Quarter-pounds and half-pounds crop up since bodyweights are converted from the "official" measurement, which is in kilos.

The same league governs amateur Free Style and Greco-Roman wrestling, which is classified as follows:

CATEGORY	WEIGHT (in pounds)
Heavyweight	Over 191
Light-Heavyweight	174¼–191
Middleweight	160¾–174
Welterweight	147¾–160½
Lightweight	136¾–147½
Featherweight	125¾–136½
Bantamweight	114½–125¾
Flyweight	Up to 114½

The Martial Arts

Centuries ago, Japanese peasants wore belts simply to hold up their wide, baggy trousers. Today, those trousers and tunics—known collectively as *gi*—are the official wardrobe of *karatekas,* the practitioners of karate. And the belt does more than keep their pants from falling down! By color, they indicate the proficiency of the martial artist—the *kyu* grades through which he or she has passed. The belts grow darker with the wearer's experience, and are awarded after passing various proficiency tests. From the novice to the expert:

COLOR
Red
White
Yellow
Green
Purple
Brown
Black

When you attain a black belt, you are officially allowed to instruct others in martial arts techniques. Once a black belt, a practitioner no longer advances in *kyu* grades, but enters the *dan* rankings, which has nine grades. (He retains his black belt for each grade he advances to.) The dan belts in karate rise from black to red-and-white to white. After rising to ninth *dan* the owner goes back to wearing beginner's red, signifying that in knowing all, he/she is ready to begin learning something new.

Judo, literally "the soft way," is a martial arts form that involves holding and throwing an opponent. Its levels are, from novice to expert:

COLOR	RANK
White	Sixth kyu
Yellow	Fifth kyu

COLOR	RANK
Orange	Fourth kyu
Green	Third kyu
Blue	Second kyu
Brown	First kyu

Some U.S. schools use only two colors: white (six through four) and brown (three through one). The numbers are reversed for the *dan* levels. From the lowest, these are black (one through five), black or white (six through eight), and black or red (nine).

The art of tae kwon do is similar to karate, but originated in Korea rather than Japan. The gradations of the "way of the foot and fist" are measured in *kup* grades, and are rated from least to most experienced as follows:

KUP	BELT COLOR
Tenth	White
Ninth	White with yellow fringe
Eighth	Yellow
Seventh	Yellow with green fringe
Sixth	Green
Fifth	Green with blue fringe
Fourth	Blue
Third	Blue with red fringe
Second	Red
First	Red with black fringe

Upon becoming a first *kup*, the next step up is to first *dan*. As in karate, the highest level one can achieve is ninth *dan*.

TIME

Units of Time

Do your kids ever ask, "What's the next measure of time after a year?" And do you answer knowingly—maybe even a little smugly—"a decade"? If you do, you're missing a lot that goes on in-between.

BREAKDOWN OF TIME
(from the shortest to the longest)
1. Second
2. Minute
3. Hour
4. Day (24 hours is technically known as a *nychthemeron*)
5. Week (or *sennight*)
6. Fortnight (two weeks)
7. Month
8. Trimester (three months; also known as a *raith*, from the Scottish)
9. Year
10. Biennium (two years)
11. Triennium (three years)
12. Quadrennium, or olympiad (four years)
13. Lustrum (five years)
14. Decade (or *decennium*)
15. Score (or *vicennium*)
16. Century
17. Millennium (or *chiliad*)

If you want to know the breakdowns for seconds, see "Mathematical Prefixes," page 135.

There are no noun forms for certain adjectives like "biduous," which means lasting for two days, or "enneatic," occurring every nine years, so those terms are not listed here. Likewise, don't assume that because there are bi-, tri-, and quadrennia, there's a quintennium. It's not so!

For the record, anything relating to "yesterday" is properly referred to as "hesternal"; to the day before that, as "nudiustertian."

Periods of Time

Now that you know the noun forms, let's dip into the adjectives relating to time.

PERIOD	MEANING
1. Semidiurnal	Twice a day
2. Diurnal	Daily
3. Semiweekly	Twice a week
4. Weekly	Once a week
5. Biweekly	Once every other week
6. Triweekly	Every three weeks
7. Monthly	Once every month
8. Bimonthly	Once every other month
9. Quarterly	Four times a year
10. Semiannual or biannual	Twice a year
11. Annual	Once a year
12. Biennial	Once every other year
13. Triennial	Once every three years
14. Quadrennial	Once every four years
15. Quinquennial	Once every five years
16. Sexennial	Once every six years
17. Septennial	Once every seven years
18. Octennial	Once every eight years
19. Novennial	Once every nine years
20. Decennial	Once every ten years
21. Undecennial	Once every eleven years
22. Duodecennial	Once every twelve years
23. Quindecennial	Once every fifteen years
24. Vicennial	Once every twenty years
25. Tricennial	Once every thirty years
26. Quadricennial	Once every forty years
27. Semicentennial	Once every fifty years
28. Centennial	Once every one hundred years

PERIOD	MEANING
29. Sesquicentennial	Once every 150 years
30. Bicentennial	Once every 200 years
31. Quadricentennial	Once every 400 years
32. Quincentennial	Once every 500 years
33. Millennial	Once every 1,000 years

There's also *perennial,* which means occurring year after year after year.

Daily Time

Ranging from the very precise to the extremely broad, these are the landmarks and boundaries of a day:

MIDNIGHT: 12 A.M., the point where one day becomes the next; the official beginning of morning.

TWILIGHT: The first, diffused glow of sunlight, when the sun is still below the horizon.

DAYBREAK: The first appearance of the sun.

DAWN: The gradual increase of sunlight after daybreak.

NOON: 12 P.M., the dividing point between morning and afternoon.

DUSK: The gradual fading of sunlight.

SUNSET: The last traces of the sun.

TWILIGHT: The last, diffused glow of sunlight, when the sun is below the horizon

EVENING: A very elastic term, loosely defining the period between sunset and bedtime.

NIGHT: The period of darkness lasting from sunset to midnight.

For people who may be at sea, sailing into or away from the sun, the chart above is irrelevant. Their day is broken down into watches and bells.

A watch consists of four hours, the first one lasting from 12:30 A.M. to 4:30 A.M. Watches are broken down into bells, which chime on the half hour (12:30 A.M. is one bell; 1:00 A.M. is two bells; and so on). When they hit eight bells at 4:00 A.M. (and a new watch), they start all over again with one bell at 4:30.

Days of the Week

In the Judeo-Christian world, there's only one Sabbath, one day holy to one god. The ancients, however, covered all their bases by honoring a different chief deity each day of the week.

Here's who was celebrated when:

ENGLISH	LATIN	SAXON
Monday	Dies Lunae	Moon's Day
Tuesday	Dies Martis	Tiu's Day (Tie, or Tiwaz, was the Norse god of war)
Wednesday	Dies Mercurii	Woden's (Odin's) Day (Odin was the king of the Norse gods)
Thursday	Dies Jovis	Thor's Day (Thor was the Norse god of thunder and crops)
Friday	Dies Veneris	Frigg's Day (Frigg was Odin's wife, the goddess of fertility)
Saturday	Dies Saturni	Saturn's Day (Saturn was the Roman god of agriculture)
Sunday	Dies Solis	Sun's Day

The Months

The Romans didn't just earmark the days of the week for certain gods; they honored the gods, specific events, or their leader during different months as well.

Note that the Romans virtually ceased their worshipful activities during the fall. With military campaigns winding down and farmers preparing for the winter, Roman concerns were purely utilitarian—something reflected in the names of the months.

JANUARY: From the Latin *Januarius,* named after Janus, the two-faced god of doorways.

FEBRUARY: From the Latin *Februarius,* derived from *februare,* "to purify," and from the festival of purification *februa.*

MARCH: From the Latin *Martius,* after Mars, the Roman god of war and vegetation. (Spring campaigns often began in this month, making it prudent to honor the god of war.)

APRIL: From the Latin *Aprilis,* derived from *aperire,* "to open," which is what flowers do at this time of the year.

MAY: From the Latin *Maius,* derived from *maiores,* "the elders," who traditionally were celebrated during this month.

JUNE: From the Latin *Junius,* honoring the goddess Juno and *iuniores*—"young people."

JULY: Named after Julius Caesar. Prior to this, the month was known as *Quintilis,* as it was the fifth Roman month.

AUGUST: Named for Augustus Caesar. Originally known as *Sextilis.*

SEPTEMBER: From the Latin *septem,* for seven.

OCTOBER: From the Latin *octo,* for eight.

NOVEMBER: From the Latin *novem,* for nine.

DECEMBER: From the Latin *decem,* for ten.

TRANSPORTATION

Airplanes

T here are so many kinds of commercial airplanes these days that it's almost impossible to remember which is which.

If you want to avoid a crowd, have a look at the chart below before booking your next reservation. Only the jets that service U.S. cities in sizable numbers have been included.

PLANE	MAXIMUM SEATING CAPACITY
Boeing 747	498
McDonnell Douglas DC-10	380
Boeing 777	375
Lockheed L-1011 TriStar	345
Boeing 767	289
Boeing 757	196
Boeing 707-320, 707-420	189
McDonnell Douglas DC-8	189
Boeing 707	179
Boeing 720	149
Tupolev Tu-144 (Soviet SST)	140
McDonnell Douglas DC-9 Series 50	139
Boeing 727	125
McDonnell Douglas DC-9 Series 30 & 40	125
McDonnell Douglas DC-9 Series 20	119
Concorde (SST)	110

PLANE	MAXIMUM SEATING CAPACITY
Boeing 737	100
McDonnell Douglas DC-9 Series 10	90

Assigning "700" numbers to Boeing jets was not caprice on the jet maker's part. By the time they started producing jets, Boeing had already used up numbers to 499 on other models, and 500–699 were already assigned to other products. Thus, they began numbering the jets with 700. The second trio of numbers after the 700 (i.e., 320 and 420 in the 707 line) were simply variants tailored to individual customers.

If you're curious about *all* passenger planes, from the popular to the obscure (like the Embraer EMB-120 Brasilia commuter plane, to name one), Arco's *Illustrated Guide to the World's Airliners* is well worth a look.

Holding Patterns

We've all experienced it: When there are too many aircraft and too few runways, planes are placed in holding patterns, circling until there's someplace to land. Since 1981, Federal Aviation Administration policy has been not to allow planes to take off if it looks like the destination's going to be crowded. However, that doesn't always work and, when necessary, air traffic control assigns planes to one of three different stacks, each one progressively lower:

JET HOLDING PATTERN: Ranges from 30,000–35,000 feet, and is intended to keep jets away from smaller aircraft.

SECONDARY STACK: Averages 20,000 feet, and is used by propeller planes only when the Primary Stack is full.

PRIMARY STACK: For propeller planes only, the levels average 15,000 feet.

Each level of every stack is approximately two thousand feet lower than the next one up.

Vehicle Safety Standards

The U.S. government publishes many useful reports, one of which is the *U.S. Federal Motor Vehicle Safety Standard*. According to tests, the average passenger car traveling on a non-slick surface should be able to stop as follows, once the brakes have been applied full force:

SPEED (in miles per hour)	STOPPING DISTANCES (in feet)
30	57
35	74
40	96
45	121
50	150
55	181
60	216
80	405
95	607
100	673

Don't forget that the reaction time, the time it takes before you actually apply the brakes, can also eat up a lot of feet.

Ship Classifications

It doesn't matter whether you've got a sailboat, motorboat, runabout, dinghy, schooner, cabin cruiser, or fishing boat; the U.S. Coast Guard categorizes all boats by their length, not their type.

The five different groupings are:

CLASS A: under sixteen feet
CLASS 1: sixteen to twenty-six feet
CLASS 2: twenty-six to forty feet
CLASS 3: forty to sixty-five feet
CLASS 4: sixty-five feet and over.

A spokesperson for the Coast Guard has absolutely no idea why the grades start with Class A, then switch to numbers. He did suggest that numbers are international, whereas letters aren't.

Makes sense, and it's nice to know that you can sell that boat of yours through an ad in *Pravda*.

THE UNIVERSE

The Solar System
According to Pythagoras

Anyone who's suffered through algebra has a vague recollection of the Greek mathematician Pythagoras (580–496 B.C.) and his theorem about the square of a hypotenuse of a right-angled triangle being equal to the sum of the squares on the other two sides.

But while Pythagoras was spot-on with his arithmetic, his astronomy left a little to be desired; around 500 B.C., he described the solar system in a way that was enlightened for the time, but a bit *off*.

From the center outward, here's how he thought things were arranged:

CENTRAL FIRE: He believed that there was an unseen ball of flame—not the sun—at the hub of the solar system. It was from this fire, he surmised, that the stars had been flung.

ANTIKHTHON: He assumed that this world, the "Counter Earth," existed between our world and the Central Fire—otherwise, we'd be incinerated. Remarkably, Pythagoras and his chief disciples—Parmenides and Philolaus—did not explain why Antikhthon wasn't visible.

EARTH: Flying against tradition, Pythagoras bravely speculated that the world was round *and* in motion . . . not the center of the universe, as most other Greeks believed.

MOON: An orb that circled the Central Fire, not the Earth.

SUN: It, too, orbited the Central Fire and was believed to be roughly the size of Earth.

PLANETS: The five known worlds that wound through the skies just beyond the sun.

STARS: These small fires hung (*how* is not explained) from the outermost element of the solar system, which was—

THE CELESTIAL SPHERE: This solid sphere was thought to surround the solar system like a giant orange rind. Pythagoras's camp was divided as to whether oblivion or the gods lurked beyond its walls.

Fellow Greek scientist Ptolemy (A.D. 127–151) set things back even further, though, when he insisted that the order of things was Earth, Moon, Mercury, Venus, the sun, Mars, and Jupiter. It wasn't until the Polish scientist Nicolaus Copernicus came along in the late fifteenth century that the real nature of the solar system was understood.

Universal Distances

When Han Solo of *Star Wars* made the mistake of referring to a "parsec" as a measure of time instead of distance, he inadvertently set the wheels in motion for this book. Obviously, he needed a handy reference guide to set him straight on things like that! (Likewise, so did the screenwriters.)

Since "miles" and "kilometers" would become unwieldy when describing the vast distances of outer space, scientists created more appropriate measurements:

TERM	DISTANCE
Astronomical Unit (AU)	92,955,630 miles (the average distance from the earth to the sun)
Light year	62,240 AUs
Parsec	3.26 light years
Kiloparsec	1,000 parsecs
Megaparsec	1 million parsecs

Star Types

L ay observers tend to recognize stars by their brightness. Astronomers, on the other hand, classify stars according to their spectral type, which tells them, in essence, how old and how hot the stars are. They grade the stars using the Harvard system created by E.C. Pickering of Harvard University in 1890. From youngest to oldest, hottest to coolest, the kinds of stars are:

TYPE	DESCRIPTION
O	Super-hot blue stars
B	Hot blue stars
A	Blue-white stars
F	White stars
G	Yellow stars
K	Orange stars
M	Cool red stars

Our own sun is a class G star.

Another system used for grading stars is the MK chart of luminosity classes, which was devised in 1943 by astronomers W. W. Morgen and P.C. Keenan. From the brightest, these classifications and the kinds of stars they describe are:

CLASS	STAR TYPE
0	Extremely luminous supergiant stars
Ia	Luminous supergiants
Ib	Lower luminosity supergiants
II	Bright giants
III	Ordinary giants
IV	Subgiants
V	Dwarfs
VI	Subdwarfs

Planetary Distances

The paths of Neptune and Pluto intersect in such a way that Neptune is occasionally farther from the sun . . . as it is now and will be for years to come. A life form on one of these planets would see the sun as barely more than just another star in the heavens.

PLANET	MEAN DISTANCE (in miles) from the sun
Pluto	3,667,900,000
Neptune	2,795,500,000
Uranus	1,783,700,000
Saturn	887,130,000
Jupiter	483,880,000
Mars	141,730,000
Earth	93,000,000
Venus	67,240,000
Mercury	57,900,000

Among those worlds with moons (i.e., all of the planets, save for Mercury and Venus), Saturn holds the record with seventeen known satellites. Jupiter is hot on its heels with sixteen.

The Sun's Composition

It's 864,000 miles across, and you'd need 1,300,000 Earths to fill it. The sun is big, all right, but it's still subject to laws of order.

From the outermost layers to the star's interior, this is the makeup of the sun:

OUTER CORONA: The outermost part of the sun's atmosphere, stretching beyond the Earth's orbit.

INNER CORONA: The next level of the sun's atmosphere, reaching to 300,000 miles above the sun.

CHROMOSPHERE: The innermost layer of atmosphere, 9,000 miles long.

PHOTOSPHERE: The surface of the sun, and the source of our life-giving sunlight.

CONVECTION ZONE: A region of rising and falling gases, believed to be approximately 30,000 miles deep.

RADIATION ZONE: An area in which radiation rises to the surface of the sun; believed to be approximately 302,000 miles deep.

CORE: Where the thermonuclear reactions occur. Its radius may be as much as 100,000 miles across.

Meteor Showers

With apologies to Al Jolson, Lyrids aren't quite what the singer meant when he sang about *April Showers*. But the Lyrids *are* April showers . . . meteor showers, just one of the ten such displays seen during the year.

A shooting star isn't a star, but a piece of space rock, a meteoroid, which has entered the Earth's atmosphere. When friction causes it to burn, the streak it produces—the shooting star—is a meteor. Any remains that reach the ground are called meteorites.

Earth's orbit regularly intercepts swarms of meteoroids, which are also circling the sun. These produce often spectacular nighttime displays, which are named for the constellations (i.e., the point in the sky) from which they originate—Ursids for Ursa Major, Leonids for Leo, etc. These meteor showers are seen ten times during the year, and are as follows:

NAME OF SHOWER	DATES
Quadrantids	January 1–6
Lyrids	April 19–24
Eta Aquarids	May 1–8
Perseids	July 25–August 18
Orionids	October 16–26
Taurids	October 20–November 20
Leonids	November 13–17
Phoenicids	December 4–5
Geminids	December 7–15
Ursids	December 17–24

Astrological Signs

The zodiac is a belt of constellations first used for the non-science of astrology, in Mesopotamia, circa 3000 B.C. Astrologers consult the zodiac to counsel clients about allegedly opportune times for various activities. (Astrology is brilliantly riposted in an article in *Sky & Telescope* Magazine, August 1989. The piece begins with the query, "What is the likelihood that one-twelfth of the world's population is having the same kind of day?")

CONSTELLATION	PERIOD COVERED
Aquarius the Water Carrier	January 20–February 18
Pisces the Fish	February 19–March 20
Aries the Ram	March 21–April 19
Taurus the Bull	April 20–May 20
Gemini the Twins	May 21–June 21
Cancer the Crab	June 22–July 22
Leo the Lion	July 23–August 22
Virgo the Virgin	August 23–September 22
Libra the Scales	September 23–October 23
Scorpio the Scorpion	October 24–November 21
Sagittarius the Archer	November 22–December 21
Capricorn(us) the Goat	December 22–January 19

Alien Encounters

In the early 1970s, the late UFO expert J. Allen Hynek coined the following terms to describe encounters with alleged aliens or alien vessels. One of these terms served as the title of the epic 1977 motion picture.

CLOSE ENCOUNTER OF THE FIRST KIND (CE-I): Sighting of a UFO at close range, without any other physical evidence.

CLOSE ENCOUNTER OF THE SECOND KIND (CE-II): Sighting of a UFO at close range, with tangible proof.

CLOSE ENCOUNTER OF THE THIRD KIND (CE-III): Sighting of a UFO occupant.

CLOSE ENCOUNTER OF THE FOURTH KIND (CE-IV): Abduction by a UFO occupant, which usually included sexual encounters.

U.S. GOVERNMENT AND HISTORY

Dates of the States

S inger Perry Como used to have a segment on his prime time variety show devoted to the "fifty nifty United States." In case you want to continue in Perry's footsteps, here are some basics about the United States—organized by the order and year in which each state joined the union, and its ranking in terms of size (number under "size" refers to the area).

ORDER	STATE	STATEHOOD	SIZE
1.	Delaware	1787	49
2.	Pennsylvania	1787	33
3.	New Jersey	1787	46
4.	Georgia	1788	21
5.	Connecticut	1788	48
6.	Massachusetts	1788	45
7.	Maryland	1788	42
8.	South Carolina	1788	40
9.	New Hampshire	1788	44
10.	Virginia	1788	36
11.	New York	1788	30

ORDER	STATE	STATEHOOD	SIZE
12.	North Carolina	1789	28
13.	Rhode Island	1790	50
14.	Vermont	1791	43
15.	Kentucky	1792	37
16.	Tennessee	1796	34
17.	Ohio	1803	35
18.	Louisiana	1812	31
19.	Indiana	1816	31
20.	Mississippi	1817	38
21.	Illinois	1818	24
22.	Alabama	1819	29
23.	Maine	1820	39
24.	Missouri	1821	19
25.	Arkansas	1836	27
26.	Michigan	1837	23
27.	Florida	1845	22
28.	Texas	1845	2
29.	Iowa	1846	25
30.	Wisconsin	1848	26
31.	California	1850	3
32.	Minnesota	1858	12
33.	Oregon	1859	10
34.	Kansas	1861	14
35.	West Virginia	1863	41
36.	Nevada	1864	7
37.	Nebraska	1867	15
38.	Colorado	1876	8
39.	North Dakota	1889	17
40.	South Dakota	1889	16
41.	Montana	1889	4
42.	Washington	1889	20
43.	Idaho	1890	13
44.	Wyoming	1890	9
45.	Utah	1896	11

ORDER	STATE	STATEHOOD	SIZE
46.	Oklahoma	1907	18
47.	New Mexico	1912	5
48.	Arizona	1912	6
49.	Alaska	1959	1
50.	Hawaii	1959	47

Native Americans

Some thirty thousand years ago, Asian hunters followed migrating mammoths and bison across the Bering land bridge and came to North America. These men and women were the ancestors of the twenty different groups of Indians living in the Americas when the European explorers arrived—from the Eskimo-Aleuts to the Iroquois-Caddoan to the Totonac-Mayan, and so on.

Regardless of their geographical location, most of these Indians shared the same kind of social structure:

NATION (or **GROUP**): Defined by common occupation (hunters, fishers, planters), geographical location, and by a similar tongue.

TRIBE (a.k.a. **VILLAGE; BAND, FOR NOMADIC PEOPLES**): Small, autonomous settlements.

CLAN: Persons within the tribe that could trace themselves to a common ancestor. Families belonging to clans shared in child-raising and other responsibilities more closely than they did with other families in the tribe. The Iroquois called this an *ohwachira,* and traced the relationships only through the women's side of the family.

MOIETIES (a.k.a. *HALVES*): Families within the clans who vied in games or had specific duties to perform.

FAMILY: Parents and their children, along with any surviving grandparents.

FIRESIDE: Among the Iroquois only, this was a division consisting of a mother and her children.

Within each tribe, Indians of importance ranked thus:

CHIEF (a.k.a. *HEADMAN OR SACHEM*): The strongest and/or wisest man. The well-being of the tribe was foremost to him. There were two kinds of chiefs, though one man often held both titles:

Peace Chief: Men who represented the tribe in dealing with other tribes.

Warrior (a.k.a. **Tree) Chief:** Men responsible for non-political activities.

SHAMAN (a.k.a. **MEDICINE MAN**): More than just the tribal "doctor," a shaman communed with the supernatural world and implored spirits to act through him on behalf of the tribe.

FUNCTIONARY: An Indian appointed to oversee specific tasks in the tribe.

TRIBESMAN AND TRIBESWOMAN: A general member of the tribe, including braves.

ADOPTEE: A prisoner or slave who was made a member of the tribe to replace a dead Indian. Each language had a different word to describe such a person.

SLAVE: A person claimed by a war party; among the tribes of the Northwest Pacific, over one-third of the population consisted of slaves.

Interestingly, while tribesmen "outranked" tribeswomen in not having to do menial work and being allowed to partake in many honorable pursuits that were forbidden to tribeswomen—such as combat and most religious ceremonies—the women in most of these tribes had one advantage over today's liberated women: They had no problem in getting a divorce. All they had to do was set their husbands' belongings outside the door, and that was that.

Alien Immigration

In 1798 Congress passed the first Alien Act, giving the government the power to admit or deport foreign citizens for any number of reasons.
Today, the United States Immigration and Naturalization Service recognizes four classes of aliens. From those who are permitted to stay the shortest to the longest amount of time:

1. **ILLEGAL ALIENS:** People who have entered the country in secret, using false documents, or who have disregarded conditions cited in their visas. The Immigration and Naturalization Service estimates that there are presently some thirteen million illegal aliens in the United States.
2. **TEMPORARY VISITORS:** Aliens admitted by visa in order to conduct business or attend school. The time period for their stay is limited and visas must be renewed.
3. **REFUGEES:** Those who have been forced to flee their native country due to war, oppression, or other factors. There are two kinds of refugees:
   Parole: Purely temporary status, but with no set time limit.
   Conditional Entrants: Eligible for permanent resident status in two years.
4. **PERMANENT RESIDENT ALIENS:** Aliens who may stay as long as they wish, provided they update the government with their latest address every January. They have most of the rights and responsibilities of Americans, although they may not vote or hold public office. There are approximately six million permanent resident aliens.

In Canada, the rules are roughly the same, though the Ministry of Employment and Immigration refers to permanent resident aliens as *landed immigrants.*

The Secession of the States

When tensions between the North and the South reached their peak in the middle nineteenth century, the Southern states seceded. Here is the order in which they joined the Confederacy, and the order in which they were readmitted to the Union following the Civil War.

SECESSION

STATE	DATE
1. South Carolina	December 20, 1860
2. Mississippi	January 9, 1861
3. Florida	January 10, 1861
4. Alabama	January 11, 1861
5. Georgia	January 19, 1861
6. Louisiana	January 26, 1861
7. Texas	February 1, 1861
8. Virginia	April 17, 1861
9. Arkansas	May 6, 1861
10. North Carolina	May 20, 1861
11. Tennessee	June 8, 1861

READMISSION

STATE	DATE
1. Tennessee	July 24, 1866
2. Arkansas	June 22, 1868
3. Alabama	June 25, 1868
4. Florida	June 25, 1868
5. Georgia	June 25, 1868
6. Louisiana	June 25, 1868
7. North Carolina	June 25, 1868
8. South Carolina	June 25, 1868

STATE	DATE
9. Virginia	January 26, 1870
10. Mississippi	February 23, 1870
11. Texas	March 30, 1870

The Underground Railroad

Though the Constitution stipulated the abolition of the slave trade by 1808, that did not come to pass. As a result, more and more slaves began risking their lives in trying to escape to the North. Methods of getting out of the South were as desperate and dangerous as they were imaginative; some slaves had themselves placed in crates and mailed to anti-slavery allies, while others clung to the anchors or hulls of boats bound for the North.

In 1831, when a slave named Tice Davids was fleeing slave owners from Kentucky, he apparently disappeared from sight. One man remarked, "He must have gone on an underground road." The name spread in the South, but was changed by industrial-minded Northerners to the underground railroad.

The underground railroad was a route traveled on foot and horseback. It was lined with the houses of abolitionists who were glad to risk their lives and security to aid runaway slaves.

The titles of operators of the underground railroad were:

1. **PRESIDENT:** He supervised all operations. The first president was abolitionist Robert Purvis, appointed in 1838.
2. **STATIONMASTER:** Owner of a house who provided food and shelter, a.k.a. a *depot*.
3. **CONDUCTOR:** Frequently a black person, who led the way through the dark.
4. **PASSENGER:** The escaped slave, a.k.a. *freight*.

The Presidential Succession

As Amendment XXV of the Constitution provides, "In case of the removal of the President from office or of his death or resignation," the following succession will occur:

1. Vice President
2. Speaker of the House of Representatives
3. President pro tempore of the Senate
4. Secretary of State
5. Secretary of the Treasury
6. Secretary of Defense
7. Attorney General
8. Secretary of the Interior
9. Secretary of Agriculture
10. Secretary of Commerce
11. Secretary of Labor
12. Secretary of Health and Human Services
13. Secretary of Housing and Urban Development
14. Secretary of Transportation
15. Secretary of Energy
16. Secretary of Education
17. Secretary of Veterans' Affairs

By the way, each secretary has the following deputies working under him or her, from the most powerful to the least:

1. Deputy secretary
2. Under secretary
3. Assistant secretary

The one exception is the Attorney General, who is assisted by:

1. Deputy Attorney General
2. Associate Attorney General
3. Solicitor General
4. Legal Counsel
5. Pardon Attorney

The National Salute

Whenever tribute must be paid, the national salute of the U.S.—gunfire—is made in the following degrees.

NUMBER OF SHOTS	OCCASION
50	July 4, at noon, to celebrate independence
21	Arrival and departure of a president, ex-president, or president-elect, or a foreign leader or member of a royal family
19	Arrival of the vice-president, speaker of the house, cabinet members, Senate president pro tempore, governor, chief justice, U.S. or foreign ambassador, prime minister, premier; arrival and departure of secretary of any military branch, Chairman of the Joint Chiefs of Staff, various other military officials.
17	Arriving and departing of generals or admirals and assistant secretaries of the military branches. Arrival only for a chairman of a congressional committee.
15	Arrival of American or visiting foreign envoys or ministers, or for a lieutenant general or vice admiral.
13	Arrival of a rear admiral (upper half) or resident ministers.
11	Arrival of a brigadier general or rear admiral (lower half), or for American chargés d'affaires and foreign counterparts and consuls general.

The Capitalist Caste System

In 1912, when labor leader Eugene Debs ran for president on the Socialist Party ticket (for the third of five tries at the White House), his party published a chart describing the *Pyramid of Capitalist System*. It showed American society as divided into five distinct castes. From the bottom:

1. **WE WORK FOR ALL, WE FEED ALL:** The workers supporting the pyramid.
2. **WE EAT FOR YOU:** The rich eating what the workers produce.
3. **WE SHOOT AT YOU:** The soldiers ready to fire at the behest of the rich.
4. **WE FOOT YOU:** The clergy guaranteeing the workers their rewards in the next world.
5. **WE RULE YOU:** The "kings" of labor and politics who pull the strings of everyone below them.

Wilson's Fourteen-Point Program

In 1918, with victory near in World War I, President Woodrow Wilson made a speech in which he outlined a fourteen-point program that would make "the world . . . fit and safe to live in." Unfortunately, his program still has not been adopted in the modern world.

In order of importance:

1. There must be no secret diplomacy between nations.
2. There must be complete freedom of the seas.
3. International trade barriers must be removed.
4. There must be a worldwide arms reduction.
5. Colonial claims worldwide must be impartially settled.
6. There must be no foreign interference in Russian affairs.
7. Belgium must be sovereign.
8. Captured territories must be returned to France.
9. Italian boundaries must be redrawn to satisfy internal factions.
10. The Austro-Hungarian nations must be allowed autonomous rule.
11. The Balkan and Serbian nations must be given financial and trade assistance.
12. Turkey must be allowed independence from the Ottoman Empire.
13. Poland must be permitted to exist independently, with access to trade and shipping.
14. A League of Nations must be created as an international body of arbitration.

WEATHER AND THE ENVIRONMENT

Clouds

If the only water vapor you can readily identify is "fog," this list may come in handy.

CLASS	HEIGHT (in feet)
N O C T I L E S C E N T Glowing atmospheric methane	50,000
C I R R O S T R A T U S Veil-like and white	20,000–40,000
C I R R U S Thin, wispy white bands	20,000–40,000
C I R R O C U M U L U S Thin, white patches	10,000–30,000
C U M U L U S White piles and mounds	6,500–23,000
A L T O C U M U L U S Group of globs or rolls	6,500–20,000
A L T O S T R A T U S Sheets of blue or gray	6,500–20,000

CUMULONIMBUS   1,500–6,500
Tall, dark storm clouds
STRATUS   1,500–6,500
Horizontal gray sheets
NIMBOSTRATUS   up to 3,000
Low, thick rainclouds
STRATOCUMULUS
(a.k.a.
CUMULOSTRATUS)   up to 1,500
Very loosely packed

By the way, you, too, can be a weatherperson! It doesn't take any equipment; all you have to do is go outside and look up. What you see will fit one of the following categories:

CLASSIFICATION	DESCRIPTION
Clear	Nothing but blue skies or stars.
Scattered	Cotton puff-type clouds here and there; you'll still get a good tan at the beach.
Broken (a.k.a. *Partly Overcast*)	Large clouds pass over the sun or stars for several minutes at a time.
Partly Obscured	There are more clouds than clear sky.
Overcast	There's a continual haze and/or nearly complete cloud cover.
Obscured	The cloud cover is absolute, with haze to boot.

Raindrops

Clouds are comprised of extremely small droplets of moisture held aloft by air currents. However, when these droplets collide, they merge in a process known as *coalescence*. When they become heavy enough, they fall. Depending upon the warmth of the air, they reach the ground in one of the following forms, from the warmest:

1. **DRIZZLE:** Small liquid droplets
2. **RAIN:** Larger liquid droplets
3. **FREEZING DRIZZLE:** Small liquid droplets that are cold, but don't freeze until they touch a colder object on the ground.
4. **FREEZING RAIN:** Same as freezing drizzle, but the droplets are larger and colder.
5. **SLEET:** Small pellets of ice; in essence, freezing rain that solidifies before it touches an object on the ground.
6. **HAIL:** Large particles of sleet, from ¼ of an inch to four inches.
7. **SNOW:** The water vapor forms ice crystals so cold that they stick to each other *before* they begin to fall.

The Wind Scale

S ir Francis Beaufort (1774–1857) was a British admiral who wanted to standardize the wind measure and so devised the following wind scale in 1805. The Beaufort Scale applies to both land and sea.

FORCE AND DESCRIPTION	MAXIMUM WIND SPEED (mph)	WHAT YOU WILL SEE ON LAND	MAXIMUM WAVE HEIGHT (feet)
Zero: Calm		Smoke rises straight up	0
One: Light Air	1–5	Smoke drifts slightly	0
Two: Light Breeze	6–11	Breeze can be felt; weather vanes will move	1
Three: Gentle Breeze	12–19	A flag will fly "extended"	3
Four: Moderate Breeze	20–28	Dust kicked up; small branches move	5
Five: Fresh Breeze	29–38	Small trees sway	8
Six: Strong Breeze	39–49	Large branches move. (Don't try opening an umbrella!)	13
Seven: Near Gale	50–61	Trees bend; walking is difficult	20
Eight: Gale	62–74	Twigs snap; walking is impeded	25
Nine: Strong Gale	75–88	Slight structural damage	33

FORCE AND DESCRIPTION	MAXIMUM WIND SPEED (mph)	WHAT YOU WILL SEE ON LAND	MAXIMUM WAVE HEIGHT (feet)
Ten: Storm	89–102	Considerable structural damage; trees uprooted	42
Eleven: Violent Storm	103–117	Widespread damage	53
Twelve: Hurricane	117–up	Extreme damage	Unlimited

Thanks to the National Oceanic and Atmospheric Administration of Silver Spring, Maryland, for this information. NOAA also cites the top three wind warnings that signal the onset of a storm:

1. The wind suddenly changes direction after several days.
2. The wind increases in the afternoon or evening.
3. High, wispy, mare's tail clouds are visible (indicating strong winds).

Wave Heights

Winds aren't the only thing mariners have to worry about. NOAA (The National Oceanic and Atmospheric Association) uses the following terms to define the condition of lakes, seas, and oceans.

CODE	WAVE HEIGHT (in feet)	DESCRIPTION
0	0	Glassy
1	up to 1	Calm
2	1–2	Rippled
3	2–4	Slightly Choppy
4	4–8	Choppy
5	8–13	Rough
6	13–20	Very Rough
7	20–30	High
8	30–45	Very High
9	over 45	Ultra High

Small-Craft Advisory Alerts

There's one simple law of order for all sailors to remember: On the open sea, a sailboat has the right of way over a powerboat. However, *everyone* moves aside for a storm.

Before going to sea, responsible boaters always check with the National Weather Service, which issues Small-Craft Advisory alerts for wind or wave conditions. They are as follows (note: a knot is equal to 1.15 miles per hour on the land):

CONDITION	DESCRIPTION
Light Wind	6 knots or less
Gust	7–16 knots
Squall	16–32 knots
Special Marine Warning	32–34 knots
Gale Warning	34–47 knots
Tropical Storm Warning	47–63 knots
Storm Warning	48 knots and over
Hurricane Warning	64 knots and over

Light Wind, Gust, and Squall are also used to describe winds on land.

If sailors don't bother to listen to a radio, they can get a summary of weather conditions by turning their binoculars to the shore. During the day, flags are used to notify sailors of an approaching storm; at night, lights are used. Here's what they mean:

TYPE OF STORM	FLAGS	LIGHTS
Small Craft Advisory	One triangular red	Red on top, white on the bottom
Gale	Two triangular red	White on top, red on the bottom
Whole Gale (encompassing storm and tropical storm)	Square red with smaller black square inside	Two red, one atop the other

TYPE OF STORM	FLAGS	LIGHTS
Hurricane	Two flags, one atop the other, same design as Whole Gale	Red on top, white in the center, red on the bottom

Hurricanes

Just as the Richter scale measures earthquakes and the Beaufort scale measures winds, the Saffir-Simpson scale, created in 1971, defines the force of a hurricane. The intensity of the storm is described by five different categories.

CATEGORY	WIND SPEED (mph)	DAMAGE
1	74–95	Minimal: Some trees, shrubs, and mobile homes will be damaged.
2	96–110	Moderate: Trees knocked down, some damage to roofs.
3	111–130	Extensive: Large trees uprooted; homes and small buildings may be weakened.
4	131–155	Extreme: Billboards, signs destroyed; windows, doors, roofs heavily damaged; flooding for up to six miles inland; major damage to any buildings near shore.
5	Over 155	Catastrophic: Buildings razed near shore; small buildings overturned far from shore; roofs and walls of large buildings severely damaged.

The practice of naming hurricanes after women was started in 1953 by the federal weather service in conjunction with officials from the army and navy. The World Meteorological Organization took over several years later and, in 1978, began alternating male names with female names.

Names are rotated over a four- or five-year period. The names of particularly severe storms are retired, to prevent confusion among records keepers.

Tornadoes

Anyone who has seen one at work knows that tornadoes are the most ferocious storms on Earth. They are also wildly unpredictable: though the average tornado is born and dies within thirty minutes, its life span can range from under a minute to seven hours (the longest one known). A tornado's destructive swath can affect just a few hundred yards, or up to three hundred miles. Wind speed at the vortex can reach up to 300 miles per hour.

Tornadoes are graded by categories, as determined by their forward speed:

CATEGORY	SPEED (in miles per hour)
1	0 (stationary)
2	1–10
3	11–25
4	26–40
5	41–60
6	61–70
7	Over 70

After a tornado has struck, meteorologists give it a post-mortem classification, from F-0 to F-5, weakest to strongest, which takes into account its duration, forward speed, and debris pattern.

Rain Forests

The decimation of the rain forests, in large part due to the development of the land, is very much in the news—especially since the vegetation in these regions contributes significantly to Earth's breathable atmosphere.

Like jungles, these damp, fertile climates are tropical; the difference between the two is primarily in what you find on the ground. In jungles, vegetation is thickly intertwined, making passage difficult. In rain forests, the thickness of the canopy prevents much sunlight from reaching the ground, leaving the vegetation comparatively sparse.

A rain forest is broken into several layers:

1. **EMERGENT LAYER:** The tops of the tallest trees, some 160 feet from the ground, which are spaced well apart.
2. **CANOPY:** Tightly packed tops of smaller trees ranging from 60 to 120 feet tall.
3. **LOWER CANOPY:** Trees, even more tightly packed, which can prosper in the shadowy sunlight that reaches their tops, some 40 to 50 feet from the ground.
4. **UNDERSTORY:** Saplings, palms, shrubs, and other small forms of foliage that live almost entirely without light, roughly 10 to 20 feet from the ground.
5. **FLOOR:** Plants that sprout in the darkness, amidst a carpet of rotting foliage.

As many as 200 different kinds of trees and 150 kinds of plants are found in just two or three *acres* of a rain forest.

Trees

Joyce Kilmer never saw anything as "lovely as a tree," but the exterior is only part of the story. The inside of a tree is also a thing of beauty, an orderly and practical progression of layers:

1. **BARK:** The hard, dead exterior of a tree that protects the internal layers from the elements.
2. **CAMBIUM:** The region just inside the bark. The outside of this layer generates new bark; the inside produces the wood that forms the next interior layer.
3. **SAPWOOD:** The wood of the sapwood is comprised of cells that form pipes. These tubes carry the nutritious sap—a blend of soil, water, and minerals—throughout the tree.
4. **HEARTWOOD:** Plugged-up, played-out pipes that are discarded and pushed inward to form the core of the tree.

Can you actually tell the age of a tree from its rings?

Yes. The sapwood produced in the spring is almost always lighter in color than that which is formed toward the end of the season. The following spring, more light sapwood is created, followed by more darker sapwood. These light-to-dark bands are known as annual rings. Some of the largest trees have over 3,500 such rings—meaning that they are over 3,500 years old!

The Pollutant Standard Index

The Pollutant Standard Index was created by the Environmental Protection Agency and South Coast Air Quality Management District of El Monte, California, to help us recognize some man-made environmental dangers. The scale measures the amounts of pollution in parts-per-million, and has been in use nationwide since 1978.

PSI INDEX VALUE	HEALTH EFFECTS	CAUTIONARY STATUS
0	Good	None
50	Moderate	None
100	Unhealthful	None
200	Very unhealthful	Alert: elderly or ill should stay indoors and reduce physical activity.
300	Hazardous	Warning: general population should stay indoors and reduce physical activity.
400	Extremely hazardous	Emergency: all people remain indoors, windows shut, no physical exertion.
500	Toxic	Significant Harm: same as above.

Thanks to the EPA for their help. Interested readers should check out their *Guidelines for Public Reporting of Daily Air Quality—Pollutant Standard Index* for further information.

Gradations of Heat

Athletes, laborers, and soldiers are (or should be!) aware of the gradations of heat, and how they relate to outdoor physical activity.

HEAT CATEGORY	TEMPERATURE RANGE (degrees Fahrenheit)	RECOMMENDED ACTIVITIES
I	82–85	Normal.
II	85–88	Limit strenuous activities; stay out of the sun as much as possible.
III	88–90	Don't do any strenuous activities in the sun; work or play with supervisor or partner nearby.
IV	90 and above	Avoid all strenuous activity.

When engaged in outdoor activities in the heat, individuals should drink the following amounts of water each day, as determined by their level of physical exertion:

PHYSICAL ACTIVITY	AMOUNT OF WATER (in quarts)
Light	10
Moderate	11
Heavy	13

WEIGHTS AND MEASURES

Ancient Measurements

They may be obsolete, but they're interesting nonetheless—the measurements used by ancient civilizations. (Contemporary equivalents are in parentheses.)

BIBLICAL

VOLUME:
omer (4.188 quarts)

9.4 omers	=	1 bath
10 omers	=	1 ephah

There were also shekels (497 ounces) and cubits (21.8 inches).

EGYPTIAN

WEIGHT:

60 grains	=	1 shekel
60 shekels	=	1 great mina
60 great minas	=	1 talent

GREEK

LENGTH:
cubit (18.3 inches)

408 cubits	=	1 stadion

WEIGHT:
obol (.04 ounces)

6 obols	=	1 drachma
94 drachmas	=	1 mina
60 minas	=	1 talent

ROMAN

VOLUME:
amphora (6.84 gallons)

LENGTH:
cubit (17.5 inches)

415.5 cubits	=	1 stadium

WEIGHT:
denarius (.17 ounces)

Contemporary Measurements

In the Middle Ages, every district in Europe—indeed, throughout the world—had its own system of measures, making it, to say the least, confusing. Even within individual countries, where the measurements were supposedly standardized, there were problems. In England, for example, a furrow (the root word for the modern "furlong") was the length of a plowed ditch in a square, ten-acre field. Obviously, there was room for error if the field itself wasn't exactly square. The "ell" was based on the distance between the elbow and the index fingertip (and you can be sure fabric sellers preferred to use the shortest arms for ells that they could find). Likewise, a "foot" was hardly a reliable form of measuring distance.

To create order out of this chaos, the measurements were delineated by rulers (no pun intended): a foot is said to have been based on the length of Charlemagne's appendage, while a yard was the distance from King Henry I's nose to the farthest fingertip of his extended arm. However the measurements truly originated, they were fixed in England by acts of Parliament in the 1500s, and were adopted by the rest of Europe not long thereafter.

LAND DISTANCES

12 inches	=	1 foot
3 feet	=	1 yard
5½ yards	=	1 rod (a.k.a. a pole or perch)
4 rods	=	1 chain
10 chains	=	1 furlong
8 furlongs	=	1 mile
(i.e., 5280 feet)		

SEA DISTANCES

6 feet	=	1 fathom
100 fathoms	=	1 cable length
6080 feet	=	1 nautical mile

AREA MEASUREMENTS

144 square inches	=	1 square foot
9 square feet	=	1 square yard
304¼ square yards	=	1 square rod
40 square rods	=	1 rood
4 roods (not square) (i.e., 4840 square yards)	=	1 acre

VOLUME

1728 cubic inches	=	1 cubic foot
5.8 cubic feet	=	1 bulk barrel
27 cubic feet	=	1 cubic yard

WEIGHT (Troy; after Troyes, France, where it was first established)

24 grains	=	1 pennyweight
20 pennyweights	=	1 ounce
12 ounces	=	1 pound

Unfortunately, this standardized weight system didn't satisfy everyone because it was too limited. Thus, the Avoirdupois ("Goods of Weight") system was devised:

WEIGHT

27.34 grains	=	1 dram
16 drams	=	1 ounce
16 ounces	=	1 pound
100 pounds	=	1 hundredweight
20 hundredweights	=	1 ton

Not that this more modern system entirely standardized things: the avoirdupois ton is 2,240 pounds (a.k.a. a long ton), while the U.S. ton (a.k.a. a short ton) is 2,000 pounds. Confusing matters further is the metric ton, which is 2,204.62 pounds.

Yet that's not the end of the weight problem. In 1618, the London

College of Physicians decided to break troy weights into subdivisions more suitable for their finer measurements. Thus, they came up with their own system, which is rarely used today (metric weights are more common):

APOTHECARY WEIGHTS

20 grains	=	1 scruple
3 scruples	=	1 dram
8 drams	=	1 ounce
12 ounces	=	1 pound

The Metric System

The metric system was introduced in France in 1791. Keen to do away with all things reminiscent of the old regime, revolutionaries introduced the meter, which was defined as 1/10,000,000th of the quadrant of the Earth's meridian passing through Paris (in other words, 1/40,000,000th of the Earth's circumference). After two years, however, when their calculations of the Earth's circumference were proved faulty, a meter was re-described as the space between two marks made on a platinum-iridium "meter bar" called the *metre des archives*. In 1960, the meter was more precisely defined as 1,650,763.73 wavelengths of the radiation emitted in the transition of 2P10 to 5df of the nuclide krypton-86—though some of us diehards still prefer to refer to it simply as 39.3701 inches.

LENGTHS:

10 angstroms	=	1 nanometer
1000 nanometers	=	1 micrometer
1000 micrometers	=	1 millimeter
10 millimeters	=	1 centimeter
10 centimeters	=	1 decimeter
10 decimeters	=	1 meter
10 meters	=	1 dekameter
10 dekameters	=	1 hectometer
10 hectometer	=	1 kilometer
1000 kilometers	=	1 megameter

In area, 100 square meters is an are, 100 areas is a hectare, and 100 hectares is a square kilometer.

WEIGHT

1000 milligrams	=	1 gram
10 grams	=	1 dekagram
10 dekagrams	=	1 hectogram
10 hectograms	=	1 kilogram

100 kilograms	=	1 quintal
10 quintals	=	1 tonne

CAPACITY

10 milliliters	=	1 centiliter
10 centiliters	=	1 deciliter
10 deciliters	=	1 liter or 1 cubic deciliter
10 liters	=	1 dekaliter
10 dekaliters	=	1 hectoliter
10 hectoliters	=	1 kiloliter
1 kiloliter	=	1 cubic meter

Selected Bibliography

The Average American Book. Barry Tarshis. New York: New American Library, 1979.

Board Games and Table Games from Many Civilizations. R. C. Bell. New York: Dover, 1979.

The Book of Classical Music Lists. Herbert Kupferberg. New York: Penguin Books, 1988.

The Chess Competitor's Handbook. Bozidar M. Kazic. New York: Arco, 1977.

The Compass In Your Nose and Other Astonishing Facts About Humans. Marc McCutcheon. Los Angeles: Jeremy P. Tarcher, Inc., 1989.

The Complete Book of Winter Sports. Arthur Liebers. New York: Coward-McCann, 1963.

Complete Illustrated Guide to Everything Sold in Hardware Stores. Tom Philbin and Steve Ettlinger. New York: Macmillan, 1983.

The Day of the Dinosaur. John Man. New York: Park South Books, 1978.

Dictionary of Omens & Superstitions. Philippa Waring. London: Treasure Press, 1978.

Dictionary of Science. Siegfried Mandel. New York: Dell Publishing, 1975.

The Facts On File Dictionary of Science. E. B. Uvarov and Alan Isaacs. New York: Facts on File Publications, 1986.

Famous First Facts. Joseph Nathan Kane. New York: Ace Books, 1974.

The Great Song Thesaurus. Roger Lax and Frederick Smith. New York: Oxford University Press, 1989.

The Guinness Book of Answers. Middlesex, England: Guinness Publishing Ltd., 1989.

The Household Chartalog. Edited by Cheryl Solimini. New York: Collier Books, 1989.

The International Encyclopedia of Astronomy. Edited by Patrick Moore. London: Orion Books, 1987.

Man and His Gold. The Gold Information Center, 1984.

Martial Arts of the Orient. Peter Lewis. London: W. H. Smith, 1979.

Materials Handbook. George S. Brady. New York: McGraw-Hill, 1983.

Mathematical Tables and Formulae. F. J. Camm. New York: Philosophical Library, 1958.

Myths and Legends of All Nations. Herbert Spencer Robinson and Knox Wilson. Totowa, New Jersey: Littlefield, Adams, 1976.

The New American Gazetteer. George Thomas Kurian. New York: New American Library, 1983.

The New American Medical Dictionary and Health Manual. Robert E. Rothenberg. New York: New American Library, 1982.

The New Book of American Rankings. New York: FYI Information Services, Facts on File Publications, 1984.

The New York Public Library Desk Reference. New York: The New York Public Library and Stonesong Press, 1989.

1,001 Helpful Tips, Facts & Hints from Consumer Reports. Editors of Consumer Reports Books with Monte Florman. Mount Vernon, New York: 1989.

The Only Math Book You'll Ever Need. Kogelman and Heller. New York: Facts On File Publications, 1986.

Powers of Ten. Philip Morrison and Phylis Morrison. New York: Scientific American Library, 1982.

Reader's Digest Book of Facts. Pleasantville, New York: Reader's Digest Association, 1987.

Rock Climbing. Arthur B. Clarke and Ian A.R. Price. London: Barne & Jenkins, 1979.

The Scientific Companion. Cesare Emiliani. New York: John Wiley & Sons, 1988.

The Signet Encyclopedia of Wine. E. Frank Henriques. New York: New American Library, 1984.

Standard Handbook for Mechanical Engineers. Eugene A. Avallone. McGraw-Hill, 1985.

Twenty-Five Lessons in Citizenship. D.L. Hennessey. Self-published, 1989.

The Universal Almanac 1990. Edited by John W. Wright. Kansas City, Missouri: Andrews and McMeel, 1989.

U.S. Army Special Forces Medical Handbook. Boulder, Colorado: Paladin Press, 1988.

The Weather Almanac. Detroit: Gale Research Co., 1987.

Webster's Secretarial Handbook. Springfield, Massachusetts: Merriam-Webster Inc., 1983.

The World Almanac and Book of Facts 1990. New York: Pharos Books, 1989.

World Book Desk Reference Set: Tables and Formulas. Chicago: World Book Encyclopedia, Inc., 1983.

Index

Airplanes, 206–7
Alcohol
  measurements of, 50–51
  servings, 52
Alien encounters, 219
Alien immigration. *See* Immigration,
  classes of alien.
Alphabet Poem, the, 22
Alphabets
  Arabic, 126
  Greek, 126
  Hebrew, 126
Angels, hierarchies of, 170
Angles, 137
Anesthesia, stages of, 99–100
Anniversary traditions, 105–6
Army groupings, 150–51
(Here We GoRound) the Mulberry Bush
  (nursery rhyme), 23
Astrological signs, 218
Atmospheric divisions, 91
Atomic fallout, 185
Atomic particles, 182

Bees, pecking order of, 5
Billiard balls, 84
Binary system, 133–34
Biological land regions, 88

Biology classes, 1
Birthstones, 104
Blood cells, types of, 110
Boxing, weight classes, 195
Boy Scouts
  grades of, 26–27
  ranks of, 26
Brave New World, power structure, 17–18
Brain, human, 114–15
Bridge, 77
Bullfighting, 191–92
Burns, 102

Cadency, marks of, 71
Calendars
  Chinese, 64
  Hindu, 175
  Islamic, 175
  Jewish, 175
Campfire Girls, levels of, 29
Capitalistic Caste System, The, 232
Caste System, Indian, 73
Catholic Church, hierarchy of, 173–74
Cells, types of, 110
Celtic society, 65–66
Check digits, 34
Chinese sages, 61–62
CIA, leadership of, 39

Law
  international, 35
  national, 36
Library of Congress book classification
    system, 8

Mafia, ranks of, 40
Martial arts, 197–98
Mathematical prefixes, 135
Measurements
  ancient, 248–49
  contemporary, 250–52
Meteor showers, 217
Metric System, the, 253–54
Military ranks
  Civil War, 148
  Germany (WWII), 146–47
  Soviet Union, 144–45
  United States, 138–40
Minerals, 188
Mohs Scale, the. *See* Minerals
Months, the, 205
Mountain ranges, 94
Motorcycle clubs, 41
Mummification, steps in, 55–56
Music
  interpretation, 158
  notes, 156
  scale, 152
  sounds of, 156

National salute (gunfire), 231
Native Americans, social structure of,
    223
1984, power structure in, 19
Nintendo rankings, 80
Nuclear missile systems, 149
Numerals
  Arabic, 131–32
  Hindu, 130

Mayan, 129
Roman, 127–28

Oil, crude, 186
Orchestra, 155
Oven settings, 46

Periodic Table, the 176–81
pH Scale, 187
Planet of the Apes, caste system, 20
Planetary distances, 215
Planetary layers, 89–90
Poetic meter, 10
Poker hands, 78
Pollutant Standard Index, 246
Polygons, 136
Presidential succession, 229–30
Pyramids, Egyptian, 53–54
Pythagoras, astronomical system of,
    211–12

Raindrops, 236
Rain forests, 244
Reserves, the (U.S. Military), 141
Roman army, 57–58
Roman rule, 58

Salvation Army ranks, 24–25
Sand widths, 96
Savings bonds, 33
Scrabble, 82–83
Seances, stages of, 164
Seven Ages of Man, 11–12
Ship classifications, 210
Skin
  abnormal growths, 101
  layers of, 111
Small-craft advisory alerts, 240–41

About the Author

J eff Rovin has written over sixty books, including *The Encyclopedia of Superheroes, The Encyclopedia of Supervillains,* and such bestselling series as *Winning at Trivial Pursuit,* and *How to Win at Nintendo Games.* He is a contributor to such publications as *Omni, Ladies' Home Journal,* and *Mad Magazine.* He lives in rural Connecticut.